sweetly
raw
desserts

*raw vegan chocolates, cakes,
cookies, ice cream, and more*

D1597231

HEATHER PACE

QUARRY

Quarry Books
100 Cummings Center, Suite 406L
Beverly, MA 01915

quarrybooks.com • quarryspoon.com

© 2015 by Quarry Books

First published in the United States of America in 2015 by
QUARRY BOOKS, a member of
Quarto Publishing Group USA Inc.
100 Cummings Center, Suite 406-L
Beverly, Massachusetts 01915-6101
Telephone: (978) 282-9590
Fax: (978) 283-2742
www.quarrybooks.com

Visit **www.QuarrySPOON.com** and help us celebrate
food and culture one spoonful at a time!

10 9 8 7 6 5 4 3 2 1

ISBN: 978-1-59253-978-9

Digital edition published in 2015
eISBN: 978-1-62788-159-3

Library of Congress Cataloging-in-Publication Data available

Design: Laura Shaw Design/lshawdesign.com
Photography by Melissa Welsh Photography/melissawelsh.com

Printed in China

This book is dedicated to all of the
people in my life who have encouraged
me to follow my dreams and to everyone
with a sweet tooth—may you enjoy all
of the recipes in this book.

contents

welcome to my **sweetly raw** kitchen

I've had a sweet tooth my entire life. I come by it honestly, as the whole Pace family has a love for sugar. My earliest kitchen memories are of standing beside my mom while she baked chocolate chip cookies just so that I could lick the beaters. My childhood was filled with blueberry pancakes drenched in pure maple syrup that my mom made after going blueberry picking in the forest, frosty vanilla milkshakes from the lakefront restaurant in my town that is only open during the summertime, and hot chocolate with a doughnut after swimming lessons in the lake.

I no longer eat those kind of treats, but I still have a mega sweet tooth and I indulge in dessert every day. The difference is that now I eat raw vegan desserts that are made with real food, packed with nutrition, and void of most common allergens. I'm fortunate enough to have started eating this way purely by choice. At the age of fourteen, I was introduced to the idea of eating whole, fresh foods instead of packaged, pasteurized, and animal-based foods. The idea resonated with me so much that I naturally made the transition to a vegan diet and started cooking for myself.

Many people are drawn to raw food due to weight problems, allergy, or illness and have great success in healing with this diet. Regardless of your reason for wanting to make raw desserts, I'm here to show you how easy and delicious they can be.

The recipes in this book are free of gluten, dairy, eggs, grains, refined sugar, soy, and corn. It's time to throw away the notion that dessert is "bad." This style of eating is both healthy and delicious. You'll notice that your body responds differently to raw desserts than it does to regular cooked ones. You'll feel light and energetic after eating them instead of tired and heavy. Enjoy a fresh fruit pudding or parfait for breakfast, eat a superfood bar for an afternoon snack, indulge in a piece of cheesecake for dessert—and you'll probably lose a few pounds along the way. Just remember that even these desserts are a treat. Eat your veggies, too!

If you're new to the world of raw desserts, you'll be amazed at how delicious a few simple ingredients can be and you may quickly come to appreciate the taste and satisfaction of fruit and nuts as an alternative to sugary snacks. If you've been into raw food for a while, you already know what a treat you're in for with raw desserts.

Regardless of your kitchen experience and your palate, I can assure you that there are recipes in this book for you. You'll find everything from one-step desserts to more elaborate preparations that require several steps, and even some special-occasion-worthy desserts that take a few days to make. My wish for you is to play with these recipes using them as a launching pad to create versions that will suit your taste and accommodate ingredients you have on hand. Substitute an ingredient, find a new way to present a dessert, and most of all, be fearless in the kitchen. Take a risk. You never know what delicious treat you might come up with.

In my experience, raw desserts are the best introduction to raw food for most people. Share your dessert creations with friends and family, and watch their faces light up as they take a bite. When they ask what's in it, you have the perfect opportunity to tell them about raw food!

(Raw) Chocolate Kisses!

—Heather

chapter one |
from the pantry to the table

Yes, you can "have your cake and eat it, too." You can eat a raw diet—and dessert. Gone are the days when an apple or soy pudding was the only choice if you wanted a healthy treat. From our pantry of whole foods we can make tasty raw versions of *any* dessert. Once you see how great raw desserts are, you might not want to eat the cooked kind ever again.

what is a raw vegan diet?

Raw vegan food is whole, natural plant food that has not been processed, refined, or heated over 118°F (48°C), keeping its nutritional value intact. Fruits, vegetables, nuts, seeds, and sprouted grains make up a raw food diet. They are rich in vitamins, minerals, enzymes, fiber, and water, all of which are necessary for a healthy body and mind. Raw food cleanses and allows the body to heal. This often means losing excess weight and having clearer skin, more energy, better sleep, mental clarity, and improved digestion, among other benefits.

I believe a person doesn't need to be 100 percent raw to be healthy. In fact, I think few people can thrive on a completely raw diet for the long term. For a few years I sustained a raw-food diet, but my health declined and I had to add a mixture of cooked food to my diet, including animal products. For me, balance is the key.

There are many health benefits from consistently eating a high percentage of raw food, and as this book proves, raw foods are delicious, too.

a new style of food prep

I know it can seem overwhelming to think about preparing desserts or food in general with such a seemingly limited list of food categories, but rest assured the sky is the limit. To get started, you need a pantry overhaul. It's out with the old and in with the new. We don't need traditional baking supplies such as flours, sugar, oats, chocolate, anything in a tin can, margarine, dairy products, eggs, and juice that has been pasteurized (which is most juice at the store) or anything that has been cooked and processed. We will be replacing them with a new set of ingredients like dried and fresh fruits, natural sweeteners, coconut oil, nuts, seeds, spices, natural extracts, and superfoods.

ingredients

Raw food cooking will introduce you to many new ingredients—and new ways to use your old favorites.

Sweeteners

There are many natural sweeteners to choose from to make raw desserts.

Dates: Medjool dates are my favorite whole-fruit sweetener because they're easy to use, versatile, sweet, and full of fiber and nutrients. They're like chewy candies, often used in bars, crusts, brownies, and smoothies. Always pit the dates before measuring them by pulling them in half vertically and removing the pit. The date halves are incorporated into the recipe unless it specifies to chop them. If you are using dates that are slightly on the dry side and not super soft, chop them roughly after measuring before adding them to a recipe.

Coconut Sugar: Also called coconut palm sugar, this dried sap of the coconut tree comes in granular form and has a lower glycemic index (the rate at which a food raises blood sugar) than most natural sweeteners. It also contains a lot of minerals and other nutrients. It has a sweet, graham crackerlike smell and taste and is great used in cakes and cookies, and can be blended into liquid mixtures such as puddings and cheesecake fillings.

Coconut Nectar: This is the sweet sap from the coconut palm tree. It is a thick, sticky liquid sweetener that has a slight tanginess. It is high in minerals and has a low glycemic index, making it a favorable sweetener for anyone.

Agave Nectar: This is a neutral-flavored liquid sweetener from the agave cactus plant. Both raw and cooked versions can be found, so make sure to look for "raw" on the label. There has been great debate about agave in the past few years, because its composition and production method have been compared to those of high-fructose corn syrup. I personally believe in moderation and I use it, although I prefer coconut nectar or sugar because they have more health benefits. I refer to it as "agave" or "nectar" in my recipes.

Maple Syrup: This is the watery sap from the maple tree that gets boiled down to produce syrup. Even though it isn't raw, I use maple syrup because it contains a high level of minerals. I love the flavor, too. It tastes almost like caramel and butterscotch, and it pairs well with chocolate, vanilla, ginger, lemon, maca, and berries.

Maple Sugar: A dried, granulated version of maple syrup, maple sugar can be used as a substitute for coconut sugar and vice versa. You can also find maple flakes, which are crunchy and make a delicious and pretty garnish for desserts, especially ice cream.

Fresh Fruit: Fruit boosts the sweetness of desserts while adding flavor. It's important to use properly ripened fruit because the sugars have developed, making the fruit sweeter and also more digestible.

Dried Fruit: Dates may be my favorite, but all dried fruits make excellent sweeteners because the fruits' sugar is so concentrated. All dried fruit lends its own flavor to a recipe in a way that fresh fruit alone cannot add. Their chewy texture makes them perfect for bars, crusts, and balls, or they can be soaked and blended into puddings and smoothies. Dried fruits such as mango, apple, apricot, pineapple, bananas, cherries, and raisins can be used interchangeably in recipes. Dried berries are really great, too. Choose from mulberries, goji berries, blueberries, raspberries, cranberries, and strawberries. With all dried fruits and berries, be sure to buy the unsulfured kind without oils or added sugar. Sulfites are often added to dried fruit as a preservative and some people have sensitivity to it.

Lucuma Powder: This dried and powdered fruit from South America tastes like caramel and maple. It's considered a superfood due to its high level of vitamins, minerals, and fiber, and adds a unique sweetness to desserts. It can easily be blended into drinks, chocolate, pudding, ice cream, and bars. It's also the secret ingredient in my caramel sauce (page 33).

Stevia: The leaf of the stevia plant is 200 times sweeter than regular sugar. It contains no calories, has a zero glycemic index, and has no carbohydrates, making it suitable for diabetics and people with blood-sugar issues. It can be purchased in liquid and powdered form, but I have only used the liquid for the recipes in this book. It is important to note that stevia cannot be used as the only sweetener in a dessert. It doesn't provide bulk in a recipe the way other sweeteners do because only a tiny amount of stevia is needed. Also, when used in high quantities it creates a very bitter taste. I prefer to use it in conjunction with other sweeteners in order to reduce the amount of sweetener required and cut down on cost.

Xylitol: Xylitol is a naturally occurring substance in fibrous fruits, vegetables, and North American hardwood trees. It looks and tastes like sugar but without any negative side effects. It has a very low glycemic index making it suitable for diabetics. It actually helps to decrease sugar and carbohydrate cravings. It's even good for your teeth! Xylitol helps restore a proper acid/alkaline balance in the mouth, inhibiting bad bacteria and plaque formation. A lot of the xylitol on the market comes from corncobs in China, but I personally prefer to buy xylitol that comes from trees in my own country.

Cacao

The cacao bean has been highly revered by South American, Central American, and Mexican cultures for centuries for its medicinal and nutritive properties. It was even used as currency by the Aztecs. Due to its high level of nutrients and antioxidants, raw chocolate is healthy! Isn't that wonderful news? All forms of cacao are used throughout this book.

Cacao Nibs: These broken-apart cacao beans are the dark chocolate chips of raw food.

Cacao Liquor: Also known as *cacao paste*, cacao liquor is the result of grinding cacao beans into a smooth liquid that looks like melted chocolate.

Cacao Powder: Cacao powder is the result of grinding cacao beans and then removing the fat.

Cacao Butter: This is the fat removed when turning cacao beans into cacao powder. It is very hard at room temperature and needs heat in order to be melted down to liquid that can be incorporated into recipes. Cacao is bitter on its own and needs some sweetener added to it to make it taste good.

Chia Seed

This ancient seed was consumed by the Aztecs and Mayans to increase energy and stamina. Chia is high in protein and healthy fat and even contains calcium. It is so high in fiber that it keeps you full for a long time. This helps with weight loss and "regularity." Chia absorbs up to twelve times its weight in liquid so it's a good idea to mix it with liquid before consuming it so that it doesn't absorb your digestive juices. It can be blended into smoothies and mixed into cereal or pudding to provide an added boost.

Coconut

Coconut is one of the most versatile fruits used in raw dessert preparation and is one of my favorite ingredients. It comes in many forms, all of which have different tastes and textures.

Fresh Young Coconuts: Found in grocery stores and Asian markets, fresh young coconuts contain very sweet coconut water that is low in calories and high in minerals. It can be used to replace regular water in any of my recipes with a slight decrease in sweetener to compensate for its natural sweetness. Don't confuse fresh green coconuts with old brown coconuts. The water in old coconuts has generally turned sour. Young coconuts also contain "meat" or "pulp" that is soft, pliable, and jelly-like. It's perfect for puddings, ice cream, and frostings since it blends so easily into a creamy consistency.

Shredded Coconut: Dried shredded coconut comes from the old coconut and adds texture, nutrients, and flavor to crusts, cakes, cookies, and bars. It's also a great substitute for nuts in some recipes.

Coconut Butter: When shredded coconut is blended down into liquid it becomes coconut butter. Use the melted liquid amount for the recipes in this book.

Coconut Oil: The fat of the coconut is used to help "set" desserts like cheesecake, frosting, mousse, and whipped cream because it is solid at room temperature. It also adds a soft, silky mouthfeel to any dessert. Have no fear of the word "fat"! Even though coconut oil contains saturated fat, it is quickly metabolized and easily used as energy by the body. Studies show that eating coconut oil regularly actually helps *burn fat* and also assists with brain function. Be sure to purchase "virgin" coconut oil, which has not been heated and still contains all of its nutritional benefits.

Essential Oils

An essential oil is the natural aromatic compound extracted from roots, flowers, bark, seeds, stems, and other parts of plants. Since it is so highly concentrated, a few drops will go a long way in boosting flavor. Be sure to purchase food-grade oils. Some of my favorite essential oils are peppermint and orange. I use them along with fresh mint leaves and orange zest to get the best flavor.

Extracts

Liquid extracts like vanilla, almond, and hazelnut are a great way to add flavor to desserts. Be sure to purchase all natural extracts that do not have any sugar, color, or "natural flavors" added. Be sure to read the label to know what's in the extract.

the **sweet** pantry

Keep these ingredients stocked in your kitchen and you'll always be able to make dessert. It may look like a long shopping list, but all of the dry goods fit nicely into jars in your dry pantry, most fresh fruit can sit on your counter to ripen, and the rest can be kept in the freezer. And you don't have to keep *all* of it on hand; just pick a few items from each category if you're just starting out. Over time you can collect more ingredients to complete your pantry.

Dried Fruit
Apples
Apricots
Cherries
Figs
Goji berries
Mulberries
Pineapple
Raisins
Shredded coconut

Spices and Flavorings
Allspice
Almond extract
Cardamom
Cinnamon
Cloves
Fresh nutmeg
Fresh vanilla bean
Ginger powder
Hazelnut extract
Himalayan salt
Orange essential oil
Peppermint essential oil
Turmeric
Vanilla bean powder
Vanilla extract

Seeds
Chia
Flax
Hemp
Pumpkin
Sesame
Sunflower

Nut and Seed Butters
Almond
Cashew
Coconut
Macadamia

Fresh and Frozen Fruit
Apples
Avocados
Bananas
Blueberries
Lemons
Mangos
Medjool dates
Oranges
Pineapple
Raspberries
Strawberries
Young coconut

Nuts
Almonds
Cashews
Hazelnuts
Macadamia nuts
Pecans
Walnuts

Sweeteners
Agave
Coconut nectar
Coconut sugar
Lucuma
Maple sugar
Maple syrup
Stevia

Other Ingredients
Cacao butter
Cacao nibs
Cacao powder
Carob powder
Coconut oil
Maca
Psyllium hulls
Spirulina

Herbs and Spices

Fresh herbs and dried spices contribute a lot of flavor to desserts. Mint leaves add a lovely fresh taste and green color and lemon balm leaves can be used in place of lemon zest. Look for good-quality spices that don't contain any gluten or added sugar. Turmeric is a spice that's not usually associated with dessert, but it's used to add a more pronounced yellow color to banana and lemon desserts.

Maca Powder

Maca is a magical Peruvian root that has an incredibly high level of nutrients. This superfood is adaptogenic, meaning that it adapts to whatever your body needs and helps to normalize and regulate all systems of the body. It is also known to improve libido and help with fertility. You will most commonly find maca in a dried, powdered form and a little goes a long way. It has a strong malty taste that is especially lovely when combined with sweetener and cacao. It is a great addition to smoothies for an energy boost. I refer to this powder as "maca" in my recipes.

Medicine Flower Essences

Medicine flower essences are organic, cold-pressed, food-grade flavor extracts that come from fruits, nuts, and flowers. Vanilla is my favorite and used in some of the recipes in this book—use it in place of vanilla extract. You'll need less of the essence.

Mesquite

Sometimes called mesquite flour or mesquite powder, this superfood is made from the seedpods of the mesquite tree, which grows in desert climates. It is high in calcium, magnesium, potassium, iron, fiber, and antioxidants. It is slightly sweet and has a very distinct taste that is almost malty. Mesquite pairs especially great with chocolate and can be mixed into smoothies, ice cream, pudding, cakes, and bars.

Nuts and Seeds

In raw desserts, nuts and seeds are staple ingredients. They form the bulk of recipes in the same way dairy, eggs, and flour are used in traditional desserts. There are all sorts of nuts to choose from, each with different nutritional values and tastes.

Be sure to buy *raw* nuts and seeds. A lot of nuts on the market have been heat treated in one way or another even if they are labeled raw. Cashews are heated to remove their incredibly hard shell and all American-grown almonds have been pasteurized. These nuts appear to be raw when compared to the obviously roasted ones and have had less processing and heating, so in a pinch it's fine to use regular "raw" nuts, but if you're concerned with getting the highest-quality, completely raw nuts, order from an organic raw food company.

For the best, cleanest taste in your raw desserts, use organic cashews. If you use regular "raw" ones the dessert will have a very strong cashew taste that will overpower the rest of the dessert.

Raw nut butters are great, too. I'll show you how to make them in this book, but if you're low on time you can buy butters made out of almost any nut. Make sure they are labeled "raw."

Psyllium Hulls

Psyllium hulls, also known as *husks*, are the outer coatings surrounding the seeds of several species of the plant genus *Plantago*. Often used in laxative products, they are extremely high in fiber. A small amount of psyllium goes a long way as a thickener in recipes. I particularly like using it in mousses.

Salt

I've only used Himalayan salt in the recipes in this book. This beautiful pink rock salt comes from the Himalayas and is very high in minerals. Regular salt is bleached and stripped of minerals. Every dessert *needs* at least a pinch of salt to bring out the natural flavors of the food, and some recipes call for more. Chocolate and salt go especially great together. These days it's easy to find Himalayan salt at most grocery stores and all health food stores.

Teeccino

If you like coffee but are trying to drink less of it or quit it completely, Teeccino is the perfect replacement. It's a blend of roasted and ground nuts, fruits, grains, and herbs that tastes like coffee without caffeine. It is brewed the same way as coffee and comes in several delicious flavors: original, vanilla, chocolate, and hazelnut. You can use any flavor for the recipes in this book. My favorite is hazelnut.

Vanilla Bean Powder

This is simply whole vanilla beans dried and powdered. It has incredible vanilla flavor and is a good option to keep on hand instead of or in addition to whole vanilla beans, which are more expensive and require more preparation to use.

Wild Jungle Peanuts

Most peanuts on the market have been roasted, and the raw ones contain a mold called *aflatoxin*, which is an allergen. Wild jungle peanuts grown in the Amazon are raw and free of mold. They have a delicious earthy taste and a striped purple and reddish-colored skin. Don't expect it to taste like roasted peanut butter, though. It's got a slightly bitter taste to it, but I enjoy it.

equipment and tools

While it might look like a lot of equipment is required to make raw desserts, there are really only a few basic things you'll need to start off with. A high-speed blender, food processor, spatula, knife, cutting board, microplane, and baking pans are necessary. You can collect the rest over time. Chances are you already have tools like measuring cups, measuring spoons, and mixing bowls in your kitchen.

High-Speed Blender

This is probably the most important piece of equipment for success in your raw dessert kitchen. It allows you to turn almost any ingredient into liquid, from nuts to fruit to coconut and cacao. Even though high-speed blenders are on the pricey side, it's well worth the investment because you'll get many years of use out of it. A regular cheap blender will leave mixtures with chunky bits and grainy texture and is prone to burning out quickly. The Vitamix blender is the preferred brand among raw dessert cooks. I know many people who have gone through several blenders before finally buying a Vitamix. You may as well invest in one in the first place.

Always add liquids to the blender first to allow for easier blending, and use the tamper to push the ingredients down into the blender, especially when blending thick mixtures like cheesecake filling.

Food Processor

The food processor is the second most important piece of equipment in your raw kitchen. Its purpose is to chop and break down ingredients without turning them into liquid the way a blender does. In my experience, there are many food processor brands that do a good enough job. You don't need to get the most expensive one.

With every food processor, you'll have to stop and scrape down the sides of the bowl at least once during the grinding process as the mixture usually gets pushed away from the blade. You will need at least a 9-cup (2.1 L) processor to make the recipes in this book, and you'll only need to use the basic "S" blade that every processor comes with.

your basic **raw dessert** kitchen

Here are some of the most important tools to start with:

- High-speed blender
- Spatula
- Cutting board
- Baking pans
- Food processor
- Knife
- Mircoplane
- Measuring cups and spoons

Dehydrator

Another great investment is a good dehydrator, which is the oven and microwave of raw food. It uses warm air circulated by a fan to draw water out of food over a long period of time. It can take 24 hours or even longer to dehydrate some recipes, but the wait is worth it for a delicious batch of granola, cookies, or candied nuts.

It's important to purchase a dehydrator that has a temperature control and is square-shaped, as opposed to ring-shaped. My favorite is the Excalibur dehydrator. It comes with four, five, or nine trays. Each tray comes with removable mesh screens but you will also need reusable, nonstick dehydrator sheets, like ParaFlexx sheets, for recipes with moist and liquid mixtures. After an initial drying phase on the dehydrator sheets, the mixture can be transferred to the mesh screen, which allows air to get to it on all sides. This speeds up the drying process.

Coffee Grinder

A coffee grinder allows you to grind small amounts of dry ingredients like shredded coconut, flax and chia seeds, and coconut sugar into powder. I like to use it to grind cacao nibs down to little bits for garnishing truffles. I have also used it to grind goji berries, but you don't want to attempt to grind any ingredient that is on the moist side or it will stick to the blade.

Ice Cream Maker

While it's not totally necessary, I do recommend buying an ice cream maker. You can buy a good one for as little as $75 (£44). Most machines only take about twenty minutes of churning time to produce sorbet or ice cream of soft-serve consistency. If you're not quite sure about investing in an ice cream maker right away, you can make ice cream with your high-speed blender. It will just require a bit more work and time.

If you choose to forego an ice cream maker, follow this process: after blending the ice cream ingredients, pour the liquid into ice cube trays and freeze them for 8 to 12 hours. Blend the frozen cubes in the blender along with a few tablespoons (about 50 ml) of almond milk or water until creamy. It will be more like a soft-serve ice cream.

Knife

Every kitchen wizard needs a good knife! It makes all the difference for chopping. A proper chef's knife is great, but if the idea of a big heavy knife is intimi-

dating to you, I highly recommend using ceramic knives. They are small, light, and easy to use and they never need to be sharpened. I use a ceramic knife for about 90 percent of my chopping needs and I've *never* sharpened it! One caution: Avoid using a ceramic knife to open young coconuts, chopping blocks of cacao butter, or other tough tasks, as the knife could break. I also suggest finding a good paring knife for things like peeling apples and slicing small fruits.

Cutting Board

This may seem like a funny item for the equipment section but it's a really important addition to your kitchen. I have several different cutting boards for different uses. I prefer bamboo and plastic but it comes down to preference. Have a cutting board dedicated to desserts in order to avoid contamination by garlic, onion, or any other strong tastes.

It's good to have a few different-size cutting boards: a large or medium one when you have lots to chop and a small one for chopping a single piece of fruit, a small amount of dates, or a handful of nuts. This makes clean up faster. Why clean a big cutting board when you don't have to? It's also a good idea to buy them in different colors so you can easily distinguish the purpose of each cutting board.

Since cacao butter and water don't mix (a few drops of water can ruin an entire batch of chocolate), it's important that the cacao butter doesn't touch anything watery while it's being chopped. Keep a separate board dedicated to cacao butter.

One last thing to note is that when using a cutting board, remember to place a piece of damp paper towel or damp cloth underneath it to prevent it from sliding on the counter when chopping.

Nut Milk Bag

This is a fine-mesh bag for making nut, seed, or coconut milks. It is reusable and only needs a good rinse to wash it before hanging to dry. You can also make fresh juice with a nut milk bag by blending any fruit or veggies into liquid in a high-speed blender and pouring it through the bag.

Mixing Bowls

Mixing bowls of various sizes are a good thing to have on hand. Glass and metal bowls are my favorite, but find what works for you. Glass bowls that come with lids are nice for refrigeration. Otherwise, you have to use plastic wrap.

Springform Pans

Also known as cheesecake pans, these round pans are necessary for making raw cheesecakes and layered cakes. These are many sizes of springform pans but in this book I've used 4-, 6-, 7- and 9-inch (10, 15, 17.5, and 23 cm) pans. If you have a pan that's not exactly the right size, it's fine. It will just result in a slightly thicker or thinner cake.

Pie and Tart Pans

I like to use glass pie pans. I've used a 9-inch (23 cm) pan for all the recipes in this book. You could use an 8-inch (20 cm) pan and end up with a little extra crust and filling for a "chef's treat."

Tart pans are similar to pie pans but they have a fluted edge. Be sure to get one with a removable bottom or you'll never get the tart out in one piece. They come in various sizes and shapes but I use round 4-inch (10 cm) and 8-inch (20 cm) tart pans for the recipes in this book.

Any of the pie recipes can be made into tarts and vice versa. Just be sure to use a similar-size pan.

Mini Muffin Pan and Paper Cups

A mini muffin pan makes it easy to form raw cupcakes. Paper cups are inserted into each space and the dough gets pressed in and formed to look like the baked version.

Silicone Muffin Cups

These are great for several uses and are one of my favorite kitchen gadgets. The muffin cups come in individual minis and individual large versions as well as attached in a unit of six. I use all three types for different desserts. They're all great for making cupcakes, the individual mini cups are great for making chocolates, and I like the mini ones and unit of six for making personal-size cheesecakes.

The cups are reusable, are easy to clean (in warm soapy water), can be frozen, and are easy to peel off any dessert or chocolate.

8-inch (20 cm) Square Pan

These pans are the best for making bars, brownies, and single-layer cakes. I also like to use this size pan for chilling whipped cream and frosting due to its large flat surface, which aids in "setting" the liquid more quickly than it would in a bowl.

Be sure to use a glass pan instead of nonstick metal versions to avoid toxic chemicals flaking into your food.

Silicone Chocolate Molds

There are several kinds of chocolate molds on the market: silicone, polycarbonate, and plastic. I personally prefer silicone because it can be peeled away from the chocolate effortlessly and there are countless shapes and sizes to choose from. However, it doesn't give the chocolate a shine the way the other molds do. Feel free to play with all styles of molds to find what you like.

Microplane

Also called a rasp, this fine, handheld grater is used to zest citrus and grate fresh nutmeg, ginger, and chocolate. I also like it for grating macadamia nuts to sprinkle over desserts. It's much easier to use than a regular citrus zester.

Offset Spatulas

Both a mini and a regular-size offset spatula will help your kitchen efforts. They are practical and will make your desserts look better. The mini offset spatula is used to evenly spread cheesecake fillings and frostings. It's also great for lifting cake, pie, or bars out of a pan. A large offset spatula is excellent for frosting cakes. It can swipe the entire top of the cake and then be used to frost the sides.

Spatula

A spatula's flexible surface helps scrape everything out of a blender, bowl, or food processor. You will need at least one of these. I use one for savory food and several for desserts, in different styles and sizes.

Whisk

A wire or silicone whisk is required for making raw chocolate and other recipes in this book. I also keep a mini whisk on hand for small things.

Parchment Paper

Freshly made chocolate and cookies are placed on this special nonstick paper while they set. They will easily peel off.

Baking Sheets

Any size baking sheets (also called cookie sheets) will do. Line each with a piece of parchment paper and scoop cookie dough, chocolate-covered bars, cake pops, or chocolates right onto it to set.

Flour Sifter

We won't be using this for flour in our raw dessert kitchen. Instead, it's for sifting cacao powder for making chocolate, which is important because you don't want lumpy chocolate. It's also good for sifting powders like lucuma and maca.

Squirt Bottles

A squirt bottle is not necessary, but it is great for drizzling sauces over desserts for beautiful presentation. I have three: one for chocolate sauce, one for strawberry sauce, and one for caramel sauce. You can buy them cheaply at a dollar store.

Piping Bag and Tips

Piping bags are an excellent tool for making your desserts even more beautiful. Pipe frosting, whipped cream, or chocolate ganache with various "tips" on the end to get a different look. You can get sturdy reusable bags, or you can get more inexpensive plastic piping bags that won't last as long. I've done away with the expensive ones and now I buy a package of about ten plastic bags at a time and dispose of them after a few uses. (They can be washed in warm soapy water.) The tips will keep forever.

If you don't want to bother with buying piping bags, you can use a plastic zip-top baggie and snip a little piece of the corner off. It won't look quite as nice but it will do the trick in a pinch.

Plastic Wrap

Plastic wrap is great for covering an open bowl in the fridge or wrapping around a finished dessert.

Pots

A small and medium-size pot are necessary for making chocolate and come in handy for melting cacao butter, coconut oil, and coconut butter. You'll only be putting water into the pot and placing a bowl or jar of the butter or oil in it to gently melt.

Sucker Sticks

Another extra to have in your kitchen are sucker sticks for making cake pops. Depending on how often you use them, one package will last a while.

Rolling Pin

A heavy wooden rolling pin is great for rolling out cookies and is also used for the cake roll recipe (page 44).

a fully stocked
raw dessert kitchen

4-inch (10 cm), 6-inch (15 cm), 7- or 8-inch (18 or 20 cm), and 9-inch (23 cm) springform pans
8-inch (20 cm) square pan
9-inch (23 cm) pie plate
Baking sheet
Coffee grinder
Cutting board
Dehydrator
Food processor
Glass liquid measuring cup
High-speed blender
Ice cream maker
Knife
Large offset spatula
Large tart pan
Measuring cups
Measuring spoons
Microplane
Mini muffin pan
Mini paper muffin cups
Mini tart pans
Mixing bowls of different sizes
Nut milk bag
Parchment paper
Paring knife
Pastry bag with tips
Plastic wrap
Pot
Rolling pin
Sifter
Silicone chocolate molds
Silicone muffin cups
Small offset spatula
Spatulas
Squirt bottles
Sucker sticks
Whisk

chapter two |
making it without baking it

While there are definite differences between preparing traditional cooked desserts and raw vegan desserts, there are some commonalities, too. Once you start making raw desserts you'll quickly see how easy it is and how accessible the ingredients and tools are in today's health-conscious world. Instead of baking, you'll be freezing, chilling, or dehydrating to get the same result. You'll be using the stove top to melt ingredients like cacao butter, coconut butter, and coconut oil, but at very low temperatures. And you'll be swapping out beaters and a regular blender for a food processor and high-speed blender.

Get carried away with a Tropical Parfait, page 130.

tips for success

Forget using a coffee grinder for coffee beans. In raw-food preparation you'll be using it to grind ingredients like coconut sugar, cacao beans, and flaxseeds. If you're already equipped to do a lot of baking, you'll notice that you already have a lot of the necessary tools for making raw desserts, too. Things like cookie sheets, parchment paper, measuring cups and spoons, mixing bowls, graters, offset spatulas, whisks, and springform pans are used in both kinds of dessert preparation. This will make the transition even easier.

Following are some helpful hints that are sure to assist you in your raw dessert kitchen.

Read the entire recipe before making it.
This is the very first thing I learned in culinary school. Sometimes there are several steps involved in making these recipes, so it's good to know what you have to soak, melt, thaw, or prep beforehand.

Taste as you go.
Never rely solely on a recipe because your ingredients and your tastes are probably a little different from mine. Once you have finished blending or mixing something, taste it and decide whether it needs a touch more sweetener or perhaps lemon or vanilla. Maybe a pinch of salt is needed to pop the flavors more. If a chocolate recipe is too sweet for you, add more cacao powder.

Be daring!
Try something new and out of your comfort zone. You never know what flavors you'll come to appreciate and you may discover recipes and techniques that are easier than you thought they would be.

Quality is extremely important.
Make sure the ingredients you buy are fresh and, ideally, organic. Rancid nuts will create an off taste in your desserts, as will any other bad ingredient.

Invest in basic tools.
Using a high-speed blender and food processor will ensure success in making raw desserts. You won't be able to achieve the same results with a regular blender, nor will a blender substitute for a food processor. Fortunately, these tools will last a very long time, so it's worth investing the extra money in the beginning.

sweetly raw techniques

In raw dessert preparation we won't be doing any baking. Instead, we achieve the same results by chilling cakes, pies, puddings, and chocolates in the fridge or freezer; sometimes a dehydrator is used to "bake" things such as cookies, bars, and granola.

Measuring
For success with my recipes, it's important to measure with accuracy. Making ingredient substitutions is one thing, but changing measurements can throw off a recipe, causing it not to set properly.

Cacao butter, coconut oil, and coconut butter are always measured in their liquid state. This is to be assumed for all recipes calling for them. Measure all ingredients right to the top of the measuring cup. When dates are called for, they're always to be pitted before measuring and always measured before chopping and using. The weight of young coconut pulp ranges from 125 g to 215 g per cup, depending on how firm or soft and watery it is, so I've given an average weight of 170 g for 1 cup in my recipes.

When measuring powders, scoop the spoon or cup into the powder, making sure the powder fills the cup (ensure there are no air pockets by giving it a little jiggle), and use a knife or your finger to scrape the top until the ingredient is level with the measuring spoon or cup.

Temperature
Ingredients need to be at room temperature (or close to it) before incorporating them into a recipe

that contains temperature-sensitive foods like cacao butter, coconut oil, and coconut butter. Otherwise, the whole mixture will seize. When using frozen fruit, make sure it is completely thawed and left out at room temperature for a while before blending it with temperature-sensitive ingredients. If you know you'll be using maple syrup, leave it out on the counter for several hours before making the recipe.

Melting

Cacao butter, coconut butter, and coconut oil need to be melted to a liquid state in order to incorporate them into a recipe. There are several ways to do this.

Dehydrator: Scoop coconut oil into a bowl and place the bowl into a dehydrator set to 115°F (45°C). Follow the same method for cacao butter and coconut butter but chop it into small chunks first.

Double Boiler: Fill a small pot with water and place it on the stove over very low heat. Place the butter or oil into a bowl and set it on the pot of hot water. (Do not let the bowl touch the water.) Allow it to slowly melt, stirring occasionally.

Solar Power: Melt it in a bowl in the sun!

Chilling

Along with dehydration, chilling is a primary method for "baking" raw desserts. Chilling sets a filling, allowing puddings and mousses to firm up, and turns liquid into ice cream.

For best results, I recommend chilling most things in the freezer for several hours before transferring them to the fridge. This gives a jumpstart to the chilling process and can mean the difference between a cake firming up or staying soft.

Dehydrating: The Raw Oven

There are a handful of recipes in this book that call for a dehydrator but it's a handy item to have, especially for preparing nuts and seeds.

It's important to start dehydrating at a temperature of 145°F (63°C) for the first hour of dehydration.

This boosts the drying process and prevents bacteria and mold from forming, which can happen when food is dried at a temperature that is too low and takes too long to dry. After the first hour, the dehydrator is always turned down to 115°F (46°C) until the food is dry. The Excalibur Dehydrator Company has done extensive testing of this method and the results show that nutrition and enzymes are not compromised.

Using a mini or large offset spatula helps with spreading mixtures on the dehydrator sheets.

Preparing Nuts and Seeds

I recommend soaking nuts and seeds before using them in order to release their enzyme inhibitors and make them more digestible. This process also removes bitterness and makes them taste better!

Different nuts and seeds require different soaking times. And cashews, Brazil nuts, macadamia nuts, and hemp seeds don't have any enzyme inhibitors, so they don't need to be soaked. In fact, soaking cashews turns them gray and almost fuzzy. Chia and flax seeds are gelatinous when soaked so they are treated differently than other nuts and seeds. Chia can be soaked for as little as a few hours, but I prefer it after it has soaked for 12 hours and had a proper chance to swell. Follow this process to soak and dehydrate most nuts and seeds:

1. Rinse and then soak nuts and seeds for the appropriate time in enough fresh water to completely cover them, plus an extra 1 or 2 inches (2.5 to 5 cm) because the nuts will expand.

2. Drain and then rinse the nuts using a strainer, until the water runs clear. At this point, use the soaked nuts or proceed to the next step.

3. Spread the nuts in one layer on a mesh dehydrator screen.

4. Dehydrate at 145°F (63°C) for 1 hour and then turn the temperature down to 115°F (46°C) and continue dehydrating for 18 to 20 hours for

soaking times for
nuts and seeds

Almonds: 8 to 12 hours
Brazil nuts: Do not soak.
Cashews: Do not soak.
Chia seeds: 30 minutes to 12 hours
Flax seeds: 4 to 8 hours
Hazelnuts: 8 to 12 hours
Macadamia nuts: Do not soak.
Pecans: 4 to 6 hours
Pumpkin seeds: 6 to 8 hours
Sunflower seeds: 5 to 6 hours
Walnuts: 6 to 8 hours

seeds and 20 to 24 hours for nuts, or until completely dry and crunchy. Eat one to make sure it is dry and if not, continue drying a longer.

Because nuts and seeds are such a big part of the raw food pantry, I have a few more hints for you:

* Store nuts and seeds in the fridge or freezer because they are prone to going rancid quickly, and don't buy more than you can use in the period of a few months. If you plan on using a lot of nuts and seeds in a short period of time, buy them in bulk from a raw food company in order to cut down on costs.

* If you're not using a high-speed blender in a particular recipe, grind nuts in a food processor before incorporating them into a recipe. This will allow for a smoother texture than would otherwise be possible with a regular blender.

* Be careful not to overprocess walnuts and pecans because their oils will be released and it will cause whatever you are making to become very oily. Instead, process them just enough to grind them and incorporate them into a recipe.

* Keep the pulp that is left over from making nut milk (page 30). It is used the way flour would be used in desserts. It's dense and moist, so I use it along with ground nuts or coconut for best results. Nut pulp can also be dehydrated until dry and then ground until fine to produce raw nut flour.

* When you are making the recipes in this book, be sure to use only *soaked* nuts and seeds when called for in the recipe; otherwise, use *soaked and dehydrated* nuts. I do a huge batch of dehydrated nuts at a time in order to always have them on hand. Of course, this is the ideal, but if you don't have time or a dehydrator, you can still make the recipes with regular raw nuts.

* Use whole, raw nuts (or walnut and pecan halves) in all of the recipes unless otherwise specified.

Storing Your Ingredients

While I recommend that nuts and seeds be kept in the fridge or freezer for ultimate freshness, keep a regular supply at room temperature in order to use them in recipes without waiting for them to warm up. Nut butters can be kept in the fridge or at room temperature for a shorter period of time.

Dried fruit (including dates), superfood powders (unless otherwise specified on the label), vanilla beans, sweeteners, spices, extracts, cacao powder, cacao liquor, and cacao butter can all be kept in a dry pantry at room temperature. Coconut butter and coconut oil can be stored at room temperature for many months and probably even longer. (This is why it's important not to use any water when making coconut butter. If you did, it would go bad quickly.)

Most fresh fruit should be kept at room temperature, including citrus, apples, bananas, pineapple, papaya, mango, avocados, and watermelon. They won't ripen in the fridge. Fruit is ripe when it has developed a stronger fruity smell, becomes heavier and becomes slightly soft to the touch. Once it is ripe, transfer it to the fridge to preserve it longer. Avocados respond especially great to this and will keep for about 10 days when properly ripened and then stored in the fridge crisper. I always keep a rotation of avocados on hand so that I have some on the counter and ripe ones in the fridge.

Store fruit in the freezer in sealed freezer bags only once it is ripe. Make sure bananas are spotted before peeling and freezing them. Frozen fruit will freeze forever, although I only recommend storing enough for several months at a time, as it will eventually get freezer burn and the nutritional value continues to decrease over time. Young coconuts can be left at room temperature for several days before needing to be refrigerated and used within a few more days. When I get a supply of young coconuts (which isn't too often), I make sure to freeze a few for future use. Open, drain, and remove the pulp from the coconut. Transfer the pulp to a sealed container and store it in the freezer for several months. The water can be frozen, too.

Berries should always be kept in the fridge due to being highly perishable. I prefer to keep frozen berries on hand at all times for this reason, and buy fresh berries only in season unless I need them for something special like a garnish.

Substitutions

If you don't have an ingredient or don't like a certain fruit that's used in a recipe, there are some easy substitutions. Keep in mind that substitution will change the flavor of a dessert, but in many cases the result is just as fantastic. Different ingredients will also yield a different color. For example, a pink raspberry dessert will be blue if using blueberries.

Sometimes, though, there are no suitable substitutions. There is no replacement for ingredients like cacao, maca, lucuma, coconut, and mesquite.

Some quick substitutions:

Almonds: Substitute hazelnuts or Brazil nuts.

Almond butter: Substitute another nut butter.

Almond milk: Substitute another nut milk.

Apples: Substitute with pears and vice versa.

Banana: Substitute with avocado and a little sweetener in smoothies.

Berries: Substitute any berry for another.

Cacao nibs: Substitute with dark chocolate chunks and vice versa.

Cashews: Substitute macadamia nuts and vice versa.

Coconut butter: Substitute coconut oil. (Since coconut butter is naturally slightly sweet but coconut oil is not, add a bit of extra sweetener to compensate.)

Dried fruit: Substitute any other dried fruit.

Fresh fruit: Substitute the same fruit frozen. (Always measure the fruit before thawing it, as it will decrease in size as it melts.)

Mango: Substitute pineapple and vice versa.

Pecans: Substitute walnuts and vice versa.

Vanilla bean or vanilla bean powder: Substitute vanilla extract (unless otherwise specified).

You have the option of using coconut nectar, agave, or maple syrup as a sweetener. Use your own preference and discretion here as to which one you choose. Each one will contribute a slightly different taste and level of sweetness. You can experiment to find which combinations you like. In some desserts I have used specific sweeteners that will complement the recipe, such as using agave nectar because it is the most neutral-tasting sweetener.

how to store and present your raw desserts

The sky is the limit when it comes to dressing up and serving raw desserts. They're so beautiful that no one will know they're different from the regular cooked kind unless you tell them. Fortunately, most raw desserts and chocolates can be stored for a long time, especially if they're frozen, so you can always have a dessert on hand for that unexpected special occasion or when your sweet cravings hit.

Storing Dessert
Desserts will keep longer if stored properly.

* Pure dark chocolate, like molded chocolate (with no fillings), clusters, and chunks can be stored at room temperature for two months or in the fridge or freezer for even longer.

* Cakes, pies, tarts, fillings, chocolate sauce, caramel sauce, and whipped cream will keep in the fridge for five to seven days, if they aren't garnished with fresh fruit. The fruit will spoil within a few days. If you want to store a cheesecake, for example, keep it in the fridge without any fresh fruit on top and garnish it just before serving. These desserts will keep in the freezer for two months even if they have a fresh fruit garnish. Just beware that the fruit will turn mushy when thawed.

* Ice cream and frozen desserts will keep in the freezer for two to three months.

* Puddings and fruit crumbles will keep in the fridge for three to four days.

* Beverages should not be stored. They are best enjoyed immediately upon preparation.

* Dehydrated goodies like cookies, bars, granola, and buckwheat will store at room temperature for several months depending on how dry they are. Moist cookies and bars should be kept in the fridge or freezer and will keep for a several months.

Always cover desserts that are stored in the fridge; otherwise, they will take on funny tastes from whatever else is in the fridge. Store them in a sealed container or on a plate covered in plastic wrap.

Presenting Dessert
Since we eat with our eyes first, presentation is just as important as how a dessert tastes.

* Sauces look and taste great when added to a dessert. They can be drizzled on a plate underneath a piece of dessert, around the edge or they can be drizzled over the top of a whole cake, pie, brownies, or ice cream. Use a spoon or a squirt bottle to make beautiful designs.

* There are usually several options to choose from when deciding which sauce to use for a dessert.

* Chocolate sauce pairs best with desserts featuring banana, chocolate, vanilla, berries, orange, mint, maple, maca, lucuma, nuts, coconut, and caramel. Chocolate adds a lovely contrast to light-colored desserts and rich depth to chocolate desserts.

* Berry sauces go well with flavors like vanilla, berries, nuts, chocolate, coconut, citrus, pineapple, mango, and kiwi. They give a lightness and slight acidity to a rich dessert and add a pretty color.

* Caramel complements chocolate, apple, cinnamon, pear, nuts, banana, maca, lucuma, coconut, and maple.

* Garnishes add extra taste, texture, and color to desserts. They're only limited by your imagination. Some garnishes that I like to use include fresh and dried berries; cacao nibs or powder for dusting; citrus zest; shredded, flaked, or ground coconut; dehydrated buckwheat, which adds crunch but not flavor; edible flowers such as roses, pansies, violets, and nasturtiums; diced, chunked, or sliced fresh fruit; whole or chopped herb leaves, especially mint, chocolate mint, lemon balm, and lavender; ice cream; sweeteners such as maple syrup, coconut nectar, or agave; whole or chopped nuts; powders such as maca, lucuma, mesquite, and cinnamon sprinkled by hand or sifted over a dessert; and, of course, coconut whipped cream.

how to **slice a cake**

When slicing desserts, run a sharp knife under hot water for a few seconds and then dry it with a towel. The hot, clean knife will allow for a clean cut. Wash the knife after every one to two cuts into the dessert or use a paper towel or damp cloth to wipe the knife down. Pull the knife out of a cake instead of lifting out of the top.

1

2

3

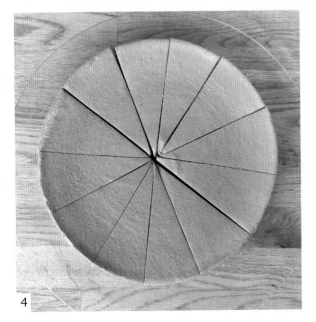

4

1. Cut the cake in half with a large knife.

2. Clean the knife between every cut using a warm, wet cloth.

3. Slice the cake into quarters, wipe the knife, and then slice diagonally from the middle of one quarter to the opposite side of the cake.

4. Cut to make more slices depending on the size of the cake: A 12-inch (30 cm) pan will yield sixteen slices, a 9- or 10-inch (23 or 25 cm) pan will yield twelve large slices, a 7- or 8-inch (18 or 20 cm) pan will yield twelve small slices, and a 6-inch (15 cm) pan will yield eight small slices.

chapter three | **everyday basics**

In this section you will find basic recipes that are
required to make some of the other recipes in this
book. Things like almond and coconut milk, nut
butters, and buckwheat crunchies can be purchased
at the store, but they're easy to make at home and
far more inexpensive, too. Other recipes, such as the
chocolate, caramel, and berries sauces, act as toppings
or complements to ice creams, cakes, and parfaits.

almond milk and almond pulp

Nut milk is so delicious, creamy, and nourishing. It's a great base for smoothies, it can be used in place of water in any of these recipes, and it's great with raw granola. Almond milk can be purchased at most grocery stores these days but there are other ingredients added and it's been pasteurized (cooked) to preserve it.

I like to stick to a ratio of 1 part soaked almonds to 3 or 4 parts water, but if you prefer a really thick milk you can use 1 part soaked almonds to 2 parts water. Use a ratio of 1 to 5 if you want to stretch your almond milk further. This recipe will work for any nut milk, although you won't need to strain through the nut milk bag when using cashews or macadamia nuts.

1 cup (145 g) soaked almonds

3 to 4 cups (705 to 940 ml) water

Blend the almonds and water in a high-speed blender until the nuts are broken down.

TIP You can make sweet vanilla almond milk by blending the milk with 2 or 3 dates and 1 teaspoon vanilla extract or ½ teaspoon vanilla bean powder.

Pour the mixture through a nut milk bag over a large bowl and gently squeeze until all of the milk has been released. Transfer the almond pulp to a sealed container and store it in the fridge for a few weeks or in the freezer for up to 2 months. Store the almond milk in the fridge for up to 6 days. Stir before using.

Yield 3 to 4 cups (750 to 1000 g)

coconut milk

Here's the easy way to have instant raw coconut milk when you don't have a fresh young coconut. Just like almond milk, you can stretch it out by adding more water, but it won't be quite as creamy if you do. Feel free to substitute this milk for the almond milk in any of the smoothie recipes.

1 cup (85 g) dried shredded coconut

2 cups (470 ml) water

Blend the coconut and water in a high-speed blender until smooth. Pour the liquid through a nut milk bag over a large bowl, and gently squeeze until all the milk has been released. Store the milk in the fridge for up to 4 days.

Yield 1¾ cups (410 ml)

how to **make nut butter**

These days, raw nut butters are widely available for purchase but they can be expensive. It only takes a food processor, nuts, and a few noisy minutes to make your own! It's ideal to use soaked, dehydrated nuts but you can use regular raw nuts and it will still turn out great.

1

2

3

4

5

3 cups (435 g) almonds or other nut

1. Process the nuts in a food processor.

2. Stop the processor to scrape down the sides.

3. Continue processing. The nuts will turn into a paste.

4. Periodically scrape down the sides. As you continue processing, the nuts will start turning to a liquid.

5. Once the butter is completely smooth and liquid, it's finished. Pour into a jar and seal.

Yield 1⅓ cups (346 g)

coconut butter

This is similar to nut butter but is made with dried coconut; it takes only a few minutes to make in a high-speed blender. Coconut butter is very hard at room temperature and needs heat to be turned back to a liquid to be incorporated into recipes.

4 to 5 cups (340 to 425 g) dried shredded coconut

Blend the coconut in a high-speed blender starting on a low speed and slowly moving to the highest speed while pushing the coconut down with the tamper. Do not add water. Continue on high speed until the coconut turns to liquid, about 2 to 3 minutes. Pour into a glass jar with a lid and store at room temperature.

Yield About 1½ cups (355 ml)

chocolate sauce

This is my all-time favorite chocolate sauce. Once chilled, the sauce firms up, so run the jar of sauce under hot water while shaking it to get the sauce to a liquid consistency again.

⅓ cup (107 g) maple syrup

¼ cup (22 g) cacao powder

2 tablespoons (28 g) almond butter

2 tablespoons (30 ml) warm water

2 tablespoons (30 ml) melted coconut oil

1 teaspoon vanilla extract

2 teaspoons (4 g) carob powder

Pinch Himalayan salt

lend all the ingredients in a blender until smooth. Store the sauce in the fridge for up to 1 week.

Yield ⅔ cup (160 g)

caramel sauce

This is a luscious caramel sauce without the sugar, cream, or butter. You can make salted caramel sauce by adding ⅛ teaspoon salt.

½ cup (120 ml) maple syrup

2½ tablespoons (35 g) almond butter

2 tablespoons (18 g) lucuma, sifted

2 tablespoons (30 ml) melted coconut butter (page 32)

1 tablespoon (15 ml) melted coconut oil

1½ teaspoons vanilla extract

2 pinches Himalayan salt

Whisk all the ingredients together in a bowl. Store in a sealed container in the fridge.

Yield 1 cup (240 g)

berry sauce and jam

This is a very basic sauce that can be used to dress up a cheesecake or drizzled on the inside of a glass before pouring in a smoothie or layering a parfait. It also doubles as the base for jam!

For the berry sauce

1½ cups (225 g) berries (if using strawberries, dice them before measuring)

3 dates

1½ teaspoons lemon juice

For the berry jam

1½ tablespoons (16.5 g) chia seeds

To make the sauce Blend all the ingredients in a blender until smooth. Add more lemon juice if desired.

To make the jam Stir the chia seeds into the berry sauce to make berry jam. Allow the mixture to thicken for at least 6 hours, ideally overnight. For a really thick jam, add an additional ½ tablespoon (5 g) of chia.

Yield ⅔ cup (200 g)

TIP With raspberries, you may want to blend and strain out the seeds before adding other ingredients.

coconut whipped cream

This silky whipped cream goes with everything. Serve it with fresh fruit, layer it in a parfait, add a dollop to a piece of pie, or pipe it onto a cake.

½ cup (120 ml) fresh coconut water

½ cup (approximately 85 g) packed young coconut pulp

⅓ cup (45 g) cashews

2 tablespoons (40 g) coconut nectar

¾ teaspoon vanilla extract

1½ teaspoons lemon juice

¼ cup + 1 tablespoon (75 ml) melted coconut oil

Blend the coconut water, coconut pulp, cashews, nectar, vanilla, and lemon juice in a blender until smooth and creamy. Add the coconut oil and blend to incorporate. Pour the cream into an 8-inch (20 cm) square pan or large flat container. Cover and chill in the fridge for at least 12 hours, or until it thickens. To boost the chilling process, put the cream in the freezer for 2 hours and then back into the fridge for at least 6 to 8 hours to set.

Yield 1½ cups (300 g)

buckwheat crunchies

Soaked and dehydrated buckwheat gets transformed into crunchy, neutral-flavored bits that make the perfect topping for ice cream and pudding and are excellent in chocolate. Buckwheat contains no wheat despite its name. In fact, it's not really a grain. It's a seed. I like to make a tray of crunchies when I'm dehydrating other things so I always have a jar of them on hand.

1 cup (120 g) raw buckwheat groats

Rinse the buckwheat and then soak it in a bowl of water for 2 to 4 hours. Make sure the water covers the buckwheat, plus about 1 inch (2.5 cm) extra. Rinse the soaked buckwheat in a strainer until the water runs clear. Spread the buckwheat on a ParaFlexx-lined dehydrator sheet. Dehydrate at 145°F (63°C) for 1 hour and then at 115°F (46°C) for 8 hours, or until dry and crunchy.

Yield ¾ cup (129 g)

how to **open a coconut**

It's quick and easy to open a young coconut. Don't be intimidated by the big knife needed, but do be careful. Use a knife with a good heel (where the knife blade meets the handle) on it or use a cleaver.

1. Turn the coconut on its side and use the knife to shave away the pointy top husk. Shave right down to the hard shell.

2. Continue shaving all the way around the coconut until the whole top of the shell is exposed.

3. Turn the coconut right side up. Holding it firmly in place on the counter with one hand, use force to whack the heel of the knife into the hard shell. It may take a few whacks to get through.

4. Once you have broken through the shell, work the knife heel into the crack and use it to pop up the top, and then set it aside.

5. Pour the coconut water into a bowl using a strainer to catch any little hard bits. Transfer it to a sealed container. The water must be clear and taste sweet. If it is pink, purple, or tastes bad, throw it out.

6. Use a large spoon to scrape the pulp out of the coconut. If the pulp is quite firm, you will have to use your strength to dig it out.

chapter four | **cakes**

For me there's nothing quite like impressing dinner guests with a gorgeous cake that is not only raw and vegan but tastes great, too. The idea of making cakes without an oven might seem funny at first but it will quickly become second nature as you work with the recipes. You'll see how easy it is to make cheesecakes, cupcakes, layer cakes, and more with only a food processor, a blender, and a fridge to chill them. Feel free to make ingredient substitutions to suit your own taste.

Try these Chocolate Cupcakes with Orange Goji Berry Frosting, page 48.

tropical cheesecake

Enjoy a little taste of the tropics even if you live far away. You can use any tropical fruit you like, and this can be made as a thick 6-inch (15 cm) cake or a slightly thinner 7-inch (18 cm) cake.

For the crust

½ **cup (72 g) almonds**

⅓ **cup (27 g) shredded coconut**

⅓ **cup (50 g) raisins**

1 teaspoon water

For the filling

1 cup (175 g) chopped, packed mango

1 cup (165 g) chopped, packed pineapple

¼ **cup + 1 tablespoon (105 g) coconut nectar**

2 tablespoons (30 ml) orange juice

2 tablespoons (30 ml) lime juice

1½ **cups (205 g) cashews**

1 tablespoon (4 g) psyllium hulls

2 teaspoons (4 g) packed orange zest

¼ **cup (60 ml) melted coconut oil**

For the sauce

2 tablespoons (30 ml) melted coconut butter (page 32)

2 tablespoons (30 ml) orange juice

1 or 2 drops stevia, optional

To make the crust Grind the almonds and coconut in a food processor. Add the raisins and process until broken down. Add the water and briefly process to combine. Press the crust into the bottom of a 6- or 7-inch (15 or 18 cm) pan.

To make the filling Combine the mango, pineapple, nectar, juices, and cashews in a blender until smooth. Add the psyllium hulls, zest, and coconut oil. Blend to incorporate. Pour the filling over the crust. Chill in the freezer for 4 to 6 hours and then transfer to the fridge for 8 hours, or until firm.

To make the sauce Whisk the ingredients together. Drizzle over the cake right before serving. It will harden quickly when chilled.

Yield 8 to 12 servings

peppermint swirl cheesecake

This cheesecake makes an excellent dessert during the holiday season. I like to present it with boughs and berries that I collect in my yard. Make the peppermint flavor as intense or as mild as you like.

To make the crust Grind the almonds into flour in a food processor. Add the remaining ingredients and process until evenly combined. Press the dough into a 6-inch (15 cm) springform pan. Set aside.

To make the filling Blend the cashews, agave, and vanilla until smooth in a blender. Add the oil, 3½ tablespoons (51 g) of the melted coconut butter, peppermint essential oil, and stevia. Blend to incorporate. Transfer ¼ cup (55 g) of the filling to a small bowl and reserve. Pour the remaining filling over the crust. In the bowl, whisk in the beet juice and remaining 1 teaspoon coconut butter into the reserved filling until combined. Pour blobs of the pink filling over the white filling. Use a chopstick or knife to push the blobs down into the filling and then swirl it around. (You can add a few extra drops of beet juice on top for more color.) Chill the cake in the freezer for 4 to 5 hours and then in the fridge for 8 to 12 hours.

Yield 8 servings

TIP To make beet juice, grate a piece of peeled beet on a microplane. Squeeze out the juice with your fingers.

For the crust

¾ cup (107 g) almonds

⅓ cup (60 g) packed dates

3 tablespoons (16 g) cacao powder

1½ teaspoons water

2 pinches Himalayan salt

For the filling

1 cup (135 g) cashews

¼ cup + 3 tablespoons (105 ml) water or almond milk (page 30)

¼ cup + 1 tablespoon (105 g) agave nectar

½ teaspoon vanilla extract

⅓ cup + 2 tablespoons (110 ml) melted coconut oil

3½ tablespoons + 1 teaspoon (58 ml) melted coconut butter, divided (page 32)

15 to 18 drops peppermint essential oil

3 or 4 drops stevia

1 teaspoon beet juice

lemon-blueberry layer cake

This beautiful cake requires a bit of time but is sure to please you and your guests! A drizzle of blueberry sauce (page 33) goes especially great with it.

For the cake

2 cups (274 g) cashews or (290 g) almonds

1 cup (80 g) shredded coconut

3 tablespoons + 2 teaspoons (15 g) xylitol, powdered

1⅓ cups (332 g) lightly packed almond pulp (page 30)

¼ cup (80 g) maple syrup

2 teaspoons (10 ml) vanilla extract

2 pinches Himalayan salt

3 tablespoons (45 ml) melted coconut oil

For the cream

1 cup (137 g) cashews or (145 g) almonds

¾ cup (177 ml) lemon juice

⅓ cup + 1½ tablespoons (145 g) agave or coconut nectar

¼ to ½ teaspoon turmeric

3 to 4 teaspoons (6 to 8 g) lemon zest

½ cup + 1 tablespoon (135 ml) melted coconut oil

For the frosting

1½ cups (222 g) blueberries

1 cup (137 g) cashews

¼ cup + ½ tablespoon (95 g) agave or coconut nectar

¼ cup (60 ml) lemon juice

⅓ cup + 2 tablespoons (110 ml) melted coconut oil

To make the cake Grind the cashews, coconut, and powdered xylitol in a food processor. If using cashews, do not over process or they will start turning buttery. They should be broken down to a fine crumb consistency. If using almonds, grind them very well. Add the pulp, maple syrup, vanilla, and salt. Process until a dough is formed. Add the coconut oil and process to incorporate. The dough will be soft and slightly sticky. Divide the dough into 3 parts. Press one part into the bottom of a 7-inch (18 cm) springform pan. Refrigerate the remaining dough.

To make the cream Blend the cashews, lemon, and nectar in a blender until smooth. Add the turmeric, zest, and oil. Blend again to incorporate. Spread half of the cream over the first layer of cake.

Freeze the cake for 6 to 8 hours, or until the cream is firm. Refrigerate the remaining cream.

To make the frosting Blend the berries, cashews, nectar, and lemon juice until smooth. Add the oil and blend to incorporate. Chill the frosting in a container in the fridge for 12 hours.

To assemble Once the first layer of lemon cream is firm, press another third of the cake dough over it. Evenly spread the remaining lemon cream over the cake layer. Set in the freezer for 6 to 8 hours, or until firm. Spread the last third of the cake dough on top. Refrigerate the cake for 4 to 6 hours before removing the ring from the springform pan. (If the cake is frozen, it will be hard to release the ring.) Spread the blueberry frosting over the cake and pipe the top.

Yield 8 to 12 servings

TIP Measure the xylitol and then powder it in a coffee grinder.

how to **frost a cake**

Frosting a cake is easier than you think. Here's how it's done.

1

2

3

4

5

1. Spoon most of the frosting on top of the cake (making sure to save about ½ cup (115 g) for piping). Use a large offset spatula to spread it evenly.

2. Push some of the frosting over the edge of the cake and use the spatula to frost the sides.

3. Fold over the top of a piping bag that has been fitted with a coupler and star tip. Carefully spoon the rest of the frosting into the bag, pushing it down toward the bottom of the bag.

4. Twist and hold the top of the bag to prevent the frosting from squishing out. Holding the bag at a slight angle, squeeze out the frosting around the top edge of the cake, moving forward and then pulling back. Continue this motion all around the perimeter of the cake.

5. Pipe around the bottom of the cake, too, and garnish as desired.

maple maca cheesecake

Maca is so healthy that we could call this cheesecake "medicine"! It can be garnished several ways. Top it with fresh figs to complement the dried figs in the crust, or drizzle it with maple syrup. I like topping it with chocolate sauce (page 32) and caramel sauce (page 33).

For the crust

½ cup (75 g) packed dried figs

½ cup (89 g) dates

1⅔ cups (200 g) walnuts

1 teaspoon water

For the filling

½ cup + 2 tablespoons (150 ml) water

⅔ cup (204 g) maple syrup

2 teaspoons (10 ml) vanilla extract

2 cups (274 g) cashews

⅛ teaspoon Himalayan salt

Scant ⅔ cup (160 ml) melted coconut oil

¼ cup (36 g) maca

To make the crust Finely chop the dried figs and dates. Combine the walnuts, figs, and dates in a food processor until they are ground to crumbs. Do not process any more or the crust will become oily. Add the water and pulse in until combined. Press into the bottom of a 9-inch (23 cm) springform pan. Set aside.

To make the filling Blend the water, syrup, vanilla, cashews, and salt in a blender until completely smooth. Add the coconut oil and maca. Blend again to incorporate (use the tamper because the mixture is thick). Pour the filling over the crust and slide the pan back and forth on the counter until the filling is even. Chill in the freezer for 4 to 6 hours and then transfer to the fridge for 8 to 12 hours, or until firm.

Yield 12 servings

orange chocolate swirl cheesecake

This swirly cake is perfect for special occasions. To offset the richness, serve it with a side of juicy orange segments.

To make the crust Grind the almonds into flour in a food processor. Add the raisins and water. Process until completely broken down. Press the crust into an 8- or 9-inch (20 or 23 cm) springform pan.

To make the filling Blend the cashews, ½ cup (170 g) of the maple syrup, ⅔ cup (160 ml) of the orange juice, and vanilla until smooth. Add the zest, coconut oil, coconut butter, and essential oil. Blend to incorporate. Transfer ⅔ cup (154 g) of the filling to a bowl and reserve. Add the cacao powder, remaining 1 tablespoon (20 g) maple syrup, and remaining 2 tablespoons (30 ml) orange juice to the remaining filling in the blender. Pour this chocolate filling over the crust. Spoon blobs of the orange filling over the top and use a chopstick to push the filling down, then swirl it around. Chill the cake in the freezer for 4 to 6 hours and then in the fridge for at least 8 to12 hours. Garnish with cacao nibs around the edge.

Yield 12 servings

For the crust

1½ cups (214 g) almonds

1 cup (145 g) raisins

2 teaspoons (10 ml) water

For the filling

2 cups (274 g) cashews

½ cup + 1 tablespoon (181 g) maple syrup, divided

⅔ cup + 2 tablespoons (190 ml) orange juice

1 teaspoon vanilla extract

2 teaspoon packed orange zest

½ cup (120 ml) melted coconut oil

¼ cup (60 ml) melted coconut butter (page 32)

4 to 8 drops orange essential oil

¼ cup + 1 tablespoon (27 g) cacao powder

cacao nibs for garnish

raspberry-vanilla cake roll

This cake roll is the perfect way to use up the almond pulp that might be collecting in your fridge. Use cashews and yellow flaxseed for a light-colored cake. For a special touch, dust agave powder over the top to look like icing sugar.

For the cake

1 cup (145 g) almonds or (137 g) cashews

⅔ cup (158 g) lightly packed almond pulp (page 30)

½ cup (89 g) dates, chopped

1 tablespoon (9 g) coconut sugar

3 tablespoons (21 g) ground flaxseed

1½ teaspoons water

½ teaspoon vanilla extract

For the cream

¾ cup (103 g) cashews

¼ cup (60 ml) water

3 tablespoons (60 g) maple syrup

1 teaspoon vanilla extract

Seeds of ½ vanilla bean

⅓ cup (80 ml) melted coconut oil

For the jam

1 cup (125 g) raspberries

3 medium dates, chopped

1½ teaspoons lemon juice

1 tablespoon + ½ teaspoon (13 g) chia seed

To make the cake Grind the almonds or cashews into fine crumbs in a food processor. Do not over process if using cashews or they will start turning to butter. Add the dates, almond pulp, and coconut sugar, and process until all ingredients are evenly combined. Add the flaxseed, water, and vanilla and pulse to combine. Set the dough in the fridge until you are ready to assemble the cake.

To make the cream Blend the cashews, water, maple syrup, and vanilla extract in a blender until smooth. Add the vanilla bean seeds and coconut oil. Blend to incorporate. Pour into a flat-bottomed container and chill in the freezer for 2 hours and then transfer to the fridge to continue chilling until firm, about 8 hours.

To make the jam Blend the berries, dates, and lemon juice in a blender or food processor until smooth. Transfer to a bowl and whisk in the chia seed. Let the mixture sit in the fridge for 8 to 12 hours, whisking periodically in the first hour to prevent the chia from clumping up.

To assemble Use your fingers to evenly press the dough on a piece of parchment paper to approximately 8 x 5 inches (20 x 13 cm). Alternatively, use a rolling pin to roll the cake dough between two pieces of parchment paper. Gently spread the vanilla bean cream evenly over the whole cake. Spread the jam over the cream. Turn the cake on the parchment paper so that the short end is facing you. Carefully roll the cake away from you, finishing with the seam side down. Some of the jelly will squish out the end. To make slicing the cake easier, chill it for a few hours first. Use a sharp knife to slice.

Yield 6 to 8 servings

how to **roll a cake roll**

Create a beautiful cake roll in six simple steps.

1. Press the dough to approximately 8 x 5 inches (20 x 13 cm) on a piece of parchment paper.

2. Use a mini offset spatula to spread the vanilla cream over the cake to the edges.

3. Spread the berry jam evenly over the cream.

4. Lift the end of the cake and parchment paper carefully starting to roll it over.

5. Roll it as tight as you can while being gentle. If any cracks form in the dough while rolling it, use your fingers to pinch it back together.

6. Slice the cake.

banana cream fudge cakes

Chocolate and banana go so great together. You can dress up these cakes however you wish. I like lots of coconut whipped cream, chocolate sauce, and sliced bananas on mine!

For the cake

1 cup (110 g) pecans

¾ cup (75 g) walnuts

½ cup (89 g) packed dates

½ teaspoon vanilla bean powder

3 tablespoons (16 g) cacao powder

⅛ teaspoon Himalayan salt

2 tablespoons (40 g) maple syrup

1 tablespoon (15 ml) melted cacao butter (page 23)

For the cream

½ cup (112 g) mashed banana

⅓ cup (45 g) cashews

2 to 2½ tablespoons (40 to 50 g) maple syrup or agave nectar

1¼ teaspoons vanilla extract

1¼ teaspoons lemon juice

Few pinches turmeric, for color

1½ tablespoons (22 ml) melted coconut butter (page 32)

¼ cup + 1½ tablespoons (75 g) melted coconut oil

For the garnish

coconut whipped cream (page 34)

sliced bananas

cacao nibs

chocolate sauce (page 32)

To make the cake Grind the nuts, dates, vanilla, cacao, and salt in a food processor until broken down to a crumbly consistency and evenly combined. Do not overprocess or the dough will become oily. Add the maple syrup and cacao butter and pulse to incorporate. Press the dough into the bottom of 6 or 7 large straight-edged silicone muffin cups.

To make the cream Blend the banana, cashews, maple syrup or agave, vanilla, and lemon juice until smooth. Add the turmeric, coconut butter, and coconut oil. Blend to incorporate.

Spread the filling over each fudge cake. Chill in the freezer for 8 to 12 hours and then peel away the silicone mold and transfer them to the fridge to thaw before serving. Dollop the cakes with coconut whipped cream, stack on some sliced banana, sprinkle with cacao nibs, and drizzle with chocolate sauce.

Yield 6 or 7 servings

chocolate cupcakes with orange goji berry frosting

These mini chocolate cupcakes are perfect for kids and great to serve at parties! Be sure to squeeze the orange juice yourself.

For the cupcakes

1⅓ cups (186 g) almonds

½ cup + 1 tablespoon (85 g) coconut sugar

⅓ cup (83 g) packed almond pulp (page 30)

¼ cup + 3 tablespoons (38 g) cacao powder

4 dates, chopped

½ teaspoon vanilla bean powder

For the frosting

3 tablespoons (20 g) goji berries

½ cup (120 ml) fresh orange juice

¾ cup (103 g) cashews

3 tablespoons (60 g) maple syrup or (80 g) coconut nectar

¼ teaspoon vanilla extract

¼ cup (60 ml) melted coconut oil

1 teaspoon packed orange zest

3 drops orange essential oil

To make the cupcakes Grind the almonds and coconut sugar down to flour in a food processor. Add the almond pulp, cacao powder, dates, and vanilla. Process until the mixture turns into a dough. Roll into 10 to 12 balls and gently press into a mini muffin cup tin lined with paper muffin cups. Shape the tops into cupcakes with your fingers.

To make the frosting Soak the goji berries in the orange juice for 15 to 20 minutes. Strain the goji berries from the juice and set them aside. Blend the orange juice, cashews, maple syrup or coconut nectar, and vanilla in a blender until smooth. Add the coconut oil, orange zest, and essential oil. Blend to incorporate. Add the goji berries and blend on low just to break them down; you can still see their color and some texture. Pour into a shallow container and chill in the freezer for 2 to 4 hours and then in the fridge for at least 10 hours. Spread or pipe the frosting over the cupcakes.

Yield 10 to 12 mini cupcakes

how to **make raw cupcakes**

Since we're not using an oven to get the cupcakes to rise, you'll need to shape them. Frosting with a piping turns them into a work of art.

1. Roll balls of dough and place them into a muffin cup–lined tray.

2. Use your fingers to shape the top of the dough, creating a small mound. Press a bit more dough on top if needed.

3. Spoon prepared frosting into a piping bag with a star tip. Twist the top and hold it in place so that no frosting squirts out. Use the fingers of the other hand to gently press the frosting down toward the tip.

4. Squeeze the bag over each cupcake, creating a swirl of icing.

mulberry-coconut cake pops

These cake pops are a great introduction to healthy eating for kids. In this version, I've featured one of my favorite dried fruits, mulberries, along with other delicious ingredients like walnuts, coconut, and hemp seeds.

½ cup (40 g) shredded coconut

½ cup (61 g) dried mulberries

½ cup (50 g) walnuts

2 tablespoons (31 g) packed almond pulp (page 30)

2 tablespoons (14 g) hemp seeds

4 dates, chopped

1½ teaspoons water

1 teaspoon vanilla extract

2 teaspoons (3 g) coconut sugar

½ batch, approximately 1¼ cups (350 g) basic dark chocolate (page 94)

Shredded coconut and chopped dried mulberries, for garnish

Grind the coconut and mulberries in a food processor until fine. Add the walnuts, pulp, hemp seeds, dates, water, and vanilla. Process until evenly combined and all ingredients are broken down. Roll the dough into ten to twelve balls. Chill in the fridge for at least 6 hours.

Dip the end of a sucker stick about ½ inch (1 cm) into the chocolate. Carefully insert a chocolate-tipped sucker stick halfway into a ball and dip each ball into the melted chocolate individually, swirling to release any excess chocolate. Hold each cake pop over an empty bowl and sprinkle shredded coconut or chopped mulberries over it. Push the stick into a piece of Styrofoam to hold the pop upright while the chocolate dries.

Yield 10 to 12 cake pops

how to **dip cake pops**

Dipping cake pops is fun. Get creative and sprinkle them with the garnishes of your choice.

1

2

3

4

1. Insert a sucker stick about ½ inch (1 cm) into melted dark chocolate and then insert the stick halfway into the cake ball.

2. Dunk the cake pop into the melted chocolate, making sure it's completely coated.

3. Once excess chocolate has dripped back into the bowl, sprinkle shredded coconut over the top.

4. Insert each cake pop into a piece of Styrofoam, allowing the chocolate to dry.

chocolate doughnuts with chocolate glaze

These are a chocolate lover's delight. Dense, rich chocolate doughnuts covered in a silky chocolate glaze and sprinkled with crunchy cacao nibs.

For the doughnuts

1 cup (145 g) almonds

⅓ cup + 1 tablespoon (59 g) coconut sugar

6 large dates, chopped

½ cup (125 g) lightly packed almond pulp (page 30)

1 teaspoon vanilla extract

¼ cup + 2 tablespoons (32 g) cacao powder

For the glaze

⅓ cup (29 g) cacao powder

¼ cup (80 g) maple syrup

1 tablespoon (16 g) almond butter

1 tablespoon (15 ml) warm water

¼ cup (60 ml) melted coconut oil

cacao nibs or shredded coconut, for garnish

To make the doughnuts Grind the almonds and coconut sugar into flour in a food processor. Add the dates, pulp, vanilla, and cacao. Grind to combine. If the dough is a bit sticky (this can depend on how moist your pulp and dates are), chill it in the fridge for a few hours before shaping. Roll the dough into 10 balls. Flatten slightly and then poke a finger through the center creating a hole. Gently shape it into a donut ring. Chill while making the glaze.

To make the glaze Place a bowl in a larger bowl of hot water to warm the bowl. Whisk the ingredients together in the warm bowl. Add extra maple syrup if desired. Dip the chilled doughnuts into the glaze and place on a parchment– or plastic wrap–lined tray. Sprinkle with cacao nibs or shredded coconut.

Yield 10 mini doughnuts

mini cinnamon cupcakes with maple cinnamon frosting

Maple, cinnamon, coconut, cashews, dates, and pecans make up these cupcakes. I don't know many other desserts that can boast such a healthy ingredient list—and they taste great, too!

To make the cupcakes Grind the cashews and coconut into crumbs in a food processor. Add additional coconut if the almond pulp is on the wet side. Add the remaining ingredients and process until broken down. Roll loosely into nine to ten balls and gently press them into a mini muffin tin lined with paper muffin cups. Shape the tops into cupcakes with your fingers.

To make the frosting Blend the cashews, water, maple syrup, vanilla, and cinnamon in a high-speed blender until smooth. Add the butter and oil and blend. Pour into a large container. Chill in the freezer for 2 to 4 hours and then in the fridge for 12 hours before spreading or piping over the cupcakes. Sprinkle extra cinnamon over the top.

Yield 9 or 10 mini cupcakes

TIP Add a few pinches of cayenne pepper for a spicy frosting.

For the cupcakes

⅔ cup (90 g) cashews

⅓ to ½ cup (27 to 40 g) shredded coconut

⅔ cup (80 g) pecans

½ cup (125 g) lightly packed almond pulp (page 30)

4 dates, chopped

¼ cup + 1 teaspoon (41 g) coconut sugar

1 teaspoon cinnamon

½ teaspoon vanilla extract

For the frosting

⅓ cup (45 g) cashews

⅓ cup (80 ml) water

2½ tablespoons (50 g) maple syrup

¼ teaspoon vanilla extract

1 teaspoon cinnamon, plus extra for sprinkling

2 tablespoons (30 ml) melted coconut butter (page 32)

2 tablespoons + 1 teaspoon (35 ml) melted coconut oil

hazelnut mocha cream cake

No one will be able to resist this creamy five-layer cake with flavors of coffee, hazelnut, and chocolate. Coffee medicine flower extract and Teeccino provide an authentic taste.

For the cake

1⅓ cups (180 g) hazelnuts

¾ cup (134 g) well-packed dates

½ cup (125 g) well-packed hazelnut pulp (page 30)

For the hazelnut cream

⅔ cup (160 ml) hazelnut milk (page 30)

1½ cups (205 g) cashews

¼ cup + 2 tablespoons (120 g) maple syrup or (125 g) agave nectar

½ teaspoon vanilla extract

1½ teaspoons hazelnut extract

¼ cup (60 ml) melted coconut oil

2 teaspoons (10 ml) melted cacao butter (page 23)

To make the cake Grind the hazelnuts into flour in a food processor. Add the dates and process until broken down. Add the pulp and process to combine. Press half of the cake into a 7-inch (18 cm) springform pan. Chill the remaining dough in plastic wrap in the fridge until needed.

To make the hazelnut cream Blend the milk, cashews, maple syrup or agave, and extracts in a blender until completely smooth. Add the oil and butter. Blend again to incorporate. Pour half of the cream over the first layer of cake. Freeze for 8 to 12 hours. Transfer the other half of the cream to the fridge for 8 to 12 hours.

To make the mocha cream Blend the Teeccino, cashews, stevia, and maple syrup or nectar until completely smooth. Add the remaining ingredients and blend until combined. Pour the cream into an 8-inch (20 cm) pan and chill in the fridge for 8 to 12 hours.

To make the milk Follow the process for making almond milk (page 30) using 1 cup (135 g) hazelnuts and 2½ cups (590 ml) water.

To assemble Spread one-third of the chilled mocha cream over the layer of hazelnut cream. Chill in the freezer for at least 4 hours. When it is firm, spread the remaining hazelnut cream evenly over the top. Freeze again until the cream is firm, about 8 hours, and then press the remaining cake dough on top. Let the cake sit at room temperature for about 1 hour, or until it is thawed enough to remove the ring. Freeze the cake again for 1 hour and while it's in the freezer, let the rest of the mocha cream sit at room temperature to soften slightly. When the cream is spreadable, spread the remaining mocha cream over the entire cake, saving a bit for piping if desired. Garnish with chocolate sauce and whole hazelnuts, if desired.

For the mocha cream

1 cup (235 ml) Teeccino

1½ cups (205 g) cashews

4 to 5 drops stevia

⅓ cup + 1 tablespoon (127 g) maple syrup or (135 g) coconut nectar

10 drops coffee medicine flower extract

¼ cup (22 g) cacao powder

¼ cup (60 ml) melted cacao butter (page 23)

3 tablespoons (45 ml) melted coconut oil

For the milk

1 cup (135 g) hazelnuts

2½ cups (570 ml) water

chocolate sauce, (page 32), optional

whole hazelnuts, optional

chapter five |
cookies, bars, and balls

For me, cookies, bars, and balls make the perfect snack whether it's with a cup of tea in the afternoon, while traveling in a car or plane, or after a workout. Since these treats are free of gluten, grains, eggs, dairy, and refined sugar, they can be enjoyed on a daily basis without any guilt. They're sure to give you a boost of energy and satisfy the 3 p.m. sugar craving.

chocolate gingerbread brownies

These brownies have to make an appearance on your holiday goody platter. A dense, spiced brownie is topped with rich chocolate frosting and garnished with cinnamon-glazed pecans.

For the brownies

1 cup (145 g) almonds

⅔ cup (120 g) packed dates

½ cup (75 g) raisins

¼ cup (22 g) cacao powder

⅔ cup (65 g) pecans

½ teaspoon vanilla extract

⅛ teaspoon Himalayan salt

2½ teaspoons (5 g) minced fresh ginger

¾ teaspoon ground ginger

½ teaspoon cinnamon

For the frosting

¼ cup (60 ml) warm water

¼ cup (38 g) coconut sugar

¼ cup (85 g) agave or coconut nectar

1 teaspoon vanilla extract

½ cup (120 ml) melted coconut butter (page 32)

⅓ cup (80 ml) melted coconut oil

⅓ cup (29 g) cacao powder

For the pecans

Slightly heaping ½ cup (55 g) chopped pecans

2½ tablespoons (50 g) maple syrup

2 tablespoons (18 g) coconut sugar

¾ teaspoon cinnamon

To make the brownies Grind the almonds into flour in a food processor. Add the dates and raisins. Grind until they are completely broken down. Add the remaining ingredients and grind until everything is evenly combined. Press the dough into an 8-inch (20 cm) square pan.

To make the frosting Blend all but the cacao powder until smooth in a blender. Add the powder and blend again. Spread the frosting over the brownies and chill in the fridge until the frosting is firm, 4 to 6 hours. Slice into 2-inch (5 cm) pieces.

To make the pecans Toss all the ingredients together in a bowl. Spoon some of the pecans over each brownie before serving.

Yield 16 brownies

nanaimo bars

Here's the raw version of a classic Canadian holiday treat. They taste better than what I remember of a regular Nanaimo bar. The vanilla medicine flower extract really makes the filling flavorful.

For the crust

1 cup (145 g) almonds

⅔ cup (54 g) shredded coconut

⅔ cup (120 g) packed dates, chopped

¼ cup (22 g) cacao powder

2 pinches Himalayan salt

1 tablespoon (15 ml) melted coconut oil

2 to 3 teaspoons (10 to 15 ml) water

For the filling

⅔ cup (90 g) cashews

½ cup (120 ml) water

¼ cup (80 g) maple syrup or (85 g) agave nectar

1 teaspoon vanilla extract

⅛ to ¼ teaspoon turmeric, for color

⅓ cup + 2 tablespoons (110 ml) melted coconut butter (page 32)

⅓ cup (80 ml) coconut oil

25 drops vanilla medicine flower extract

3 or 4 drops stevia

For the dark chocolate

¼ cup + 1 tablespoon (27 g) cacao powder

2½ tablespoons (50 g) maple syrup

¼ cup (60 ml) coconut oil

To make the crust Finely grind the almonds and coconut in a food processor. Add the remaining ingredients with 2 teaspoons (10 ml) of the water. The crust should be moist and hold together when pressed in your hand, but not sticky. If it doesn't hold together easily, add the remaining 1 teaspoon water. (Add an extra 1 tablespoon [5 g] cacao powder if you want a slightly darker chocolate crust.) Press into the bottom of an 8-inch (20 cm) square pan. Set aside.

To make the filling Blend the cashews, water, maple syrup or agave, vanilla, and turmeric until smooth and creamy. Add the coconut butter, coconut oil, vanilla, and stevia. Blend again to incorporate. Spread the cream evenly over the crust. Chill in the freezer for 3 to 4 hours and then transfer to the fridge for at least 8 hours.

To make the chocolate Whisk the ingredients together in a warm bowl. Pour the chocolate over the filling and work quickly, using a mini offset spatula to spread it before it hardens. Set the pan in the fridge for at least 30 minutes. Slice into 1½-inch (3.5 cm) bars.

Yield 20 bars

TIP To avoid cracking the chocolate, heat a sharp knife under hot water and wipe dry before slicing.

sugar cookies with lemon frosting

I have many fond memories of making sugar cookies with my mom as a child. I loved decorating them with different colored frosting. Here's a much healthier raw version. They must be stored in the fridge as they are temperature sensitive.

To make the cookies Grind the coconut and cashews into flour in a food processor. Add the remaining ingredients and process into dough. Chill the dough in the fridge for 10 to 15 minutes.

Roll the dough between 2 pieces of parchment paper and then cut cookies using a 1½-inch (3.5 cm) round cookie cutter. Carefully transfer the cookies to a parchment paper–lined tray using an offset spatula. (The dough will be slightly soft.) Chill in the fridge for at least 2 hours, or until firm.

To make the frosting Whisk together all the ingredients in a small bowl. The frosting will thicken slightly as you whisk and the coconut butter cools. Spread the frosting on the cookies using a mini offset spatula or butter knife. Chill in the fridge.

Yield 12 to 15 cookies

TIP Don't use too much turmeric in the frosting as it has a strong taste. Use just enough to get a soft yellow color.

For the cookies

1 cup (80 g) shredded coconut

1 cup (137 g) cashews

3 tablespoons (60 g) agave nectar

1½ teaspoons vanilla extract

2 pinches salt

1½ teaspoons warm water

3 tablespoons (45 ml) melted coconut oil

3 tablespoons (45 ml) melted coconut butter (page 32)

For the frosting

¼ cup + 2 tablespoons (150 ml) melted coconut butter (page 32)

¼ cup + 1 teaspoon (65 ml) lemon juice

1½ tablespoons (30 g) agave nectar

1 teaspoon packed lemon zest

Few pinches turmeric, for color

superfood balls

These balls pack a nutritional and flavorful punch! Be sure to use the orange because it adds a really fantastic flavor.

⅓ cup (43 g) almonds

⅓ cup (45 g) cashews

¼ cup (21 g) dried coconut

¼ cup (45 g) packed dates, chopped

¼ cup (30 g) dried mulberries

2 tablespoons (14 g) hemp seeds

2 teaspoons (6 g) chia seeds

3 tablespoons (20 g) goji berries

2 teaspoons (6 g) lucuma

1 teaspoon maca

¼ teaspoon vanilla bean powder or ¼ teaspoon vanilla extract

3 or 4 drops orange essential oil

1 teaspoon water, as needed

Additional lucuma or maca, for garnish

Grind the almonds, cashews, and coconut into flour in a food processor. Add the remaining ingredients and grind until they are broken down and combined. Add a bit more water if needed in order to get the dough to hold together when pressed. Roll the balls in lucuma or maca, if desired.

Yield 12 balls

chocolate chip cookies

Chocolate chip cookies were one of my favorite childhood snacks. Truth be told, I always liked eating the dough better than eating the cookies after they were baked. Now I can have my dough and eat it, too!

Grind the almonds and coconut in a food processor until finely ground. Add the cashews and grind again briefly. Add the dates, vanilla, and salt. Process until they are fully incorporated. Transfer to a bowl and stir in the chocolate chunks. Use a mini ice cream scoop to make balls. Transfer them to a parchment paper–lined tray. Chill in the fridge for at least 4 hours.

Yield 28 mini cookies

½ cup (71 g) almonds

½ cup (40 g) shredded coconut

1 cup (137 g) cashews

⅔ cup (120 g) well-packed dates, chopped

2 teaspoons (10 ml) vanilla extract

⅛ teaspoon Himalayan salt

1 to 1¼ cups (175 to 219 g) dark chocolate chunks (page 94)

key lime pie bars

These bars are sweet, creamy, tangy, and refreshing! No one will know the filling is made with avocado.

For the crust

¾ cup (60 g) shredded coconut

½ cup (71 g) almonds

⅓ cup (45 g) cashews

¼ cup (45 g) finely chopped dried mango, optional

⅓ cup (60 g) dates, chopped

½ teaspoon water

Pinch Himalayan salt

For the filling

¾ cup (172 g) mashed avocado

¼ cup + 1 tablespoon (105 g) coconut nectar

⅓ cup (80 ml) lime juice

¼ teaspoon vanilla extract

⅓ cup + 2 tablespoons (110 ml) melted coconut oil

3 tablespoons (45 ml) melted coconut butter (page 32)

2 to 3 teaspoons (10 to 15 g) lime zest

6 to 8 drops stevia

Dried coconut or mango, for garnish

To make the crust Grind the coconut and almonds into flour in a food processor. Add the cashews and mango. Grind briefly. Add the dates, water, and salt. Grind until the dates are broken down. Press the mixture into the bottom of an 8-inch (20 cm) square pan.

To make the filling For instructions on cutting an avocado, see page 151. Blend the avocado, coconut nectar, lime, and vanilla in a blender until smooth. Add the oil, butter, zest, and stevia. Blend again to incorporate. Spread the filling over the crust. Chill the bars in the freezer for 2 to 4 hours, and then in the fridge for 6 to 8 hours, or until set. Slice into 2-inch (5 cm) squares. Sprinkle with dried coconut or mango, if desired.

Yield 16 squares

TIP Be sure to finely chop the dried mango because it won't break down in the food processor.

hemp chocolate chunk blondies

These bars are the perfect power-packed pick-me-up with nuts, hemp seeds, dates, and chunks of dark chocolate. No need to reach for an unhealthy snack!

⅔ cup (86 g) almonds

⅔ cup (54 g) shredded coconut

1 cup (137 g) cashews

1 cup (178 g) well-packed dates

⅓ cup (40 g) hemp seeds

1½ teaspoons vanilla extract

1 teaspoon water

⅛ teaspoon Himalayan salt

1½ cups (262 g) dark chocolate chunks (page 94)

Grind the almonds and coconut in a food processor. Add the cashews and process briefly. Add the dates, hemp seeds, vanilla, water, and salt. Process until the dates are broken down. Transfer the dough to a bowl and fold in the chocolate chunks. Firmly press the dough into an 8-inch (20 cm) square pan. Chill in the fridge for at least 4 hours. Slice into 2-inch (5 cm) squares or slightly smaller.

Yield   16 to 20 bars

chocolate vanilla sandwich cookies

A thick vanilla cashew cream gets sandwiched between two chewy chocolate cookies in this recipe. They're irresistible.

To make the cookies Grind the almonds into flour in a food processor. Add the dates. Process until they are completely broken down. Add the remaining ingredients with 1½ teaspoons of the water and process until evenly combined. The dough must be moist and pliable enough to roll out. Add the remaining ½ teaspoon water if needed. Using a rolling pin, roll the dough to ¼-inch (6 mm) thick between 2 pieces of parchment paper and cut into rounds with a 1½-inch (3.5 cm) round cookie cutter. Press together the scraps and continue rolling and cutting until the dough is used. You should have 16 cookies. Transfer the cookies to a parchment paper–lined tray and place in the freezer for at least 1 hour before adding the filling.

To make the cream Blend the cashews, water, maple syrup, and vanilla in a blender until smooth and creamy. Add the stevia, oil, and butter. Blend again to incorporate. Chill the cream in the freezer for 2 to 4 hours and then in the fridge for 12 hours.

To assemble Place a spoonful of chilled cream onto 8 of the cookies. Gently press the second cookie on top making a sandwich. Smooth the sides with your finger or a mini offset spatula. Eat immediately or let the cookies chill in the fridge for a few hours to firm up a bit.

Yield 8 sandwich cookies

TIP You can use another ½ to 1 teaspoon vanilla extract in place of the vanilla medicine flower extract, but it will turn the filling an off-white color.

For the cookies

1 cup (145 g) almonds

⅔ cup (120 g) packed dates

3 tablespoons (16 g) cacao powder

1½ tablespoons (22 ml) melted coconut butter (page 32)

½ teaspoon vanilla bean powder

1½ to 2 teaspoons (7 to 10 ml) water

For the cream

¾ cup (103 g) cashews

¼ cup (60 ml) water

2½ tablespoons (50 g) maple syrup

20 drops vanilla medicine flower extract

½ teaspoon vanilla extract

6 drops stevia

⅓ cup + 1 tablespoon (95 ml) melted coconut oil

2 tablespoons (30 ml) melted coconut butter (page 32)

coconut macaroons

These are perfect for the coconut lover in your life. These cookies are hard on the outside but soft and chewy on the inside. Because they require a lot of dehydration time, I like to make a double batch and store them in the freezer.

1 cup (145 g) almonds

2 cups (160 g) shredded coconut

¼ cup + 2 tablespoons (120 g) coconut nectar

1 teaspoon vanilla extract

¼ teaspoon Himalayan salt

¼ cup + 2 tablespoon (90 ml) melted coconut oil

Grind the almonds into flour in a food processor. Add the remaining ingredients and process to combine. Use a mini ice cream scoop to transfer balls onto a ParaFlexx-lined dehydrator sheet. Dehydrate at 145°F (63°C) for 1 hour and continue dehydrating at 115°F (46°C) for 32 to 36 hours, transferring the balls onto the mesh screen after the first few hours of dehydrating. Dehydrate until they are firm but still soft and chewy on the inside.

Yield 30 balls

peanut butter and jelly bars

Here's a new way to enjoy a classic combo. A nutty crust is topped with a sweet, creamy peanut butter filling and spread with a layer of berry jam. You can even top them with a sprinkle of peanuts.

To make the crust Grind the almonds into flour in a food processor. Add the raisins and process until they are completely broken down. Add the water and pulse it in. Press the dough firmly into an 8- inch (20 cm) square pan. Set aside.

To make the filling In a bowl sitting over a pot of hot water, whisk all ingredients together until smooth. Spread the filling over the crust. Chill in the fridge until it firms up, 4 to 6 hours.

To make the jam Add the extra 2 teaspoons (6 g) chia to the jam. Once the jam is thick and the peanut butter filling is firm, spread the jam evenly over the top. Slice into approximately 2 x 1½-inch (5 x 3.5 cm) bars.

Yield 20 bars

For the crust

1⅓ cups (186 g) almonds

1⅓ cups (195 g) raisins

½ teaspoon water

For the filling

1 cup (260 g) raw jungle peanut butter (page 31)

⅓ cup (115 g) coconut nectar

1½ teaspoons vanilla extract

⅛ teaspoon Himalayan salt

¼ cup + 3 tablespoons (105 ml) melted coconut oil

For the jam

2 teaspoons (6 g) chia seeds

2 batches, about 1⅓ cups (420 g) berry jam (page 33)

turtle cookies

A chewy pecan cookie is topped with a mound of caramel and dipped in chocolate. They do take a bit of time to make because they require several steps and dehydration, so make a double batch.

For the cookies

⅔ cup (86 g) almonds

1 cup (100 g) pecans

½ cup (89 g) dates, chopped

2 teaspoons (10 ml) water

For the caramel

⅔ cup (120 g) well-packed dates

¼ cup (80 g) maple syrup

1½ teaspoons vanilla extract

2 pinches Himalayan salt

¼ cup + 2 tablespoons (90 ml) melted coconut oil

For assembly

1 batch, approximately 2½ cups (700 g) basic dark chocolate (page 94)

Pecans, for garnish, optional

To make the cookies Grind the almonds into flour in a food processor. Add the pecans, dates, and water. Process the dough until all ingredients are broken down. Use a rolling pin to roll the dough between 2 pieces of parchment paper to approximately ⅓- to ½-inch (8.5 to 12.5 mm) thick. Use a 1½-inch (3.5 cm) round cookie cutter to cut cookies and transfer them to a dehydrator tray. Dehydrate at 145°F (63°C) for 1 hour and then at 115°F (46°C) for 30 hours.

To make the caramel Process the dates into a paste in a food processor. Add the maple syrup, vanilla, and salt. Process briefly to combine. Add the coconut oil and process until the caramel is smooth. Chill the caramel in the fridge for at least 4 hours and then spread a thick layer over each cookie creating a slight mound. Freeze the cookies while making the chocolate.

To assemble Dip a cookie into the melted chocolate. Lift the cookie out with a fork allowing extra chocolate to drip back into the bowl, and then lightly drag the bottom of the cookie along the edge of the bowl to clean off any last excess chocolate. Place the cookie on a tray lined with parchment paper and pull the fork out from underneath. Top with pecans, if desired. Chill in the fridge for at least 20 minutes, until the chocolate hardens.

Yield 13 cookies

chapter six |
ice cream and frozen desserts

So many people are eliminating dairy these days. The good news is that you can still enjoy incredibly creamy, rich, and flavorful ice cream that uses cashew and coconut cream in place of regular cream and milk. I promise that you will be amazed at how close these recipes are to real ice cream. Turn any of these ice creams into elaborate desserts by adding any dessert toppings of your choice like brownie chunks, nuts, fruit, sauces, dehydrated buckwheat, or anything else you can think of!

vanilla bean ice cream

Here, real vanilla bean seeds are added to a cashew cream, making the ice cream rich in taste and texture. It's the perfect base for an incredible ice cream sundae. Add toppings like caramel sauce (page 33), chocolate sauce (page 32), berry sauce (page 33), and nuts or fruits of your choice.

2 cups (274 g) cashews

2 cups (475 ml) water

½ cup (161 g) maple syrup

1½ tablespoons (22 ml) vanilla extract

Seeds of 1 vanilla bean

2 pinches Himalayan salt

2½ tablespoons (37 ml) melted coconut oil

Blend all but the coconut oil in a blender until completely smooth. Add the oil and blend to incorporate. Chill the liquid in the fridge for 8 to 12 hours. Process the thick cream in an ice cream maker according to the manufacturer's instructions and then transfer it to a container and freeze for a few hours until it firms up.

Yield 4 to 6 servings

"any fruit" milkshake

As a child I loved milkshakes and blizzards. When I was about twelve years old, I started experimenting and making my own frosty ice cream shakes, adding whatever fun ingredients I could find in my parents' kitchen. I'm so happy to have a healthy raw vegan version that leaves my stomach and my taste buds feeling good. Use whatever frozen fruit you have on hand.

Blend all the ingredients in a high-speed blender until smooth and frosty. It is really thick, so add more almond milk if desired. Drink immediately.

Yield 2 servings

1 cup (235 ml) almond milk
  (page 30)

1 cup (140 g) vanilla bean ice cream
  (page 74)

1 cup (145 g) berries or diced
  frozen fruit

Few drops stevia, to taste

mocha ice cream

I really love this rich chocolate and coffee-flavored ice cream even though I'm not a coffee drinker. Dilute the Teeccino with some water, to taste, if you prefer it to be less strong and add as much or little of the coffee extract as you like.

1½ cups (350 ml) Teeccino, chilled

1½ cups (205 g) cashews

½ cup (161 g) maple syrup

2 teaspoons (10 ml) vanilla extract

⅓ cup (29 g) cacao powder

⅛ teaspoon Himalayan salt

2 tablespoons (30 ml)
   melted coconut oil

8 to 10 drops coffee medicine
   flower extract

Blend the Teeccino, cashews, maple syrup, vanilla, cacao, and salt in a blender until completely smooth. Add the coconut oil and extract. Blend to incorporate. Chill the liquid in the fridge for 12 hours. Process the cream in an ice cream maker according to the manufacturer's instructions and then transfer it to a container and freeze it for a few hours until it firms up.

Yield 6 servings

peaches n' cream ice cream

This recipe is perfect when peaches are in abundance in the summer. Still, I highly recommend using the peach medicine flower extract to boost the flavor. Layering the ice cream and the peach purée makes a beautiful swirl when you scoop it. But you could omit the extra step and simply spoon the purée over the ice cream.

For the ice cream

4½ cups (765 g) diced peaches

1½ cups (205 g) cashews

½ cup (170 g) agave or
  coconut nectar

¼ cup (60 ml) water

1½ teaspoons lemon juice

¾ teaspoon vanilla extract

9 drops peach medicine flower
  extract, optional

7 or 8 drops stevia

For the purée

2 cups (340 g) diced peaches

6 medium dates

To make the ice cream Blend all the ingredients until smooth in a high-speed blender. Taste and add more coconut nectar if needed. It should taste a bit too sweet, as the sweetness will decrease when frozen. Chill in the fridge for at least 12 hours and then process in an ice cream machine according to the manufacturer's instructions.

To make the purée Blend the peaches and dates until smooth and in a blender. Chill in the fridge for 12 hours.

To assemble Layer half of the churned peach ice cream in a flat container. Spread half of the peach purée on top. Spread the remaining ice cream on top. Spread the rest of the peach purée evenly over the top. Transfer the container to the freezer for 5 to 6 hours before scooping.

Yield 6 servings

banana soft serve

This is the classic one-ingredient raw vegan ice cream recipe. Frozen bananas are puréed down to thick, creamy ice cream in only seconds. To make flavored ice cream, add ¾ cup (37 g) frozen fruit of your choice before blending.

Process the bananas in a food processor or a high-speed blender, using the tamper, until smooth. Eat immediately.

3 large frozen bananas, roughly chopped

Yield 1 or 2 servings

TIP I always keep a rotation of bananas on hand. I like to buy ripe "baking bananas" that are on sale. When they're spotted, I peel them and transfer them to the freezer.

raspberry cardamom brownie ice cream sandwiches

Here's a healthy, colorful, dressed-up version of the vanilla and chocolate ice cream sandwiches that are so common. Raspberries, cardamom, and vanilla are a great flavor combination.

For the brownie

2 cups (290 g) almonds

1 cup (178 g) well-packed dates

1⅓ cups (195 g) raisins

½ cup (43 g) cacao powder

1 teaspoon vanilla extract

⅔ cup (80 g) walnuts

2 pinches Himalayan salt

1½ teaspoons water

For the ice cream

2¼ cups (350 g) freshly churned vanilla bean ice cream (page 74)

1½ teaspoons ground cardamom

2 cups (250 g) raspberries, lightly mashed

To make the brownie Grind the almonds into flour in a food processor. Add the dates and raisins. Process until they are completely broken down. Add all the remaining ingredients and process to combine. Press half the dough into an 8-inch (20 cm) square pan. Set aside. Refrigerate the remaining dough.

To make the ice cream sandwiches Transfer the vanilla ice cream (which will be like soft serve) directly from the ice cream maker to a bowl and quickly stir in the cardamom. Gently fold in the raspberries. Do not overmix or the raspberry color will bleed. Spread the ice cream evenly over the brownie, working quickly to prevent melting. Immediately transfer to the freezer until frozen, at least 6 hours. Firmly press the other half of the brownie dough on top. Cut into 1½ x 2½-inch (3.5 x 6 cm) bars.

Yield 15 bars

pecan praline ice cream

This ice cream is so decadent. The recipe makes two to three times more pecan praline than you'll need for the ice cream, leaving extra for snacking on, or dip it into dark chocolate (see page 97) for an extra-special treat.

¼ cup + 2 tablespoons (120 g) maple syrup

¼ cup + 2 tablespoons (56 g) coconut sugar

⅓ cup (80 ml) melted coconut butter (page 32)

¼ cup + 1 tablespoon (75 ml) melted coconut oil

1½ tablespoons (24 g) almond butter

1½ teaspoons vanilla extract

2 teaspoons (10 ml) warm water

1¾ cups (175 g) pecan halves, divided

1 batch freshly churned vanilla bean ice cream (page 74)

Blend the maple syrup, coconut sugar, coconut butter, coconut oil, almond butter, vanilla, and water in a blender until smooth. Transfer the liquid to a bowl and stir in 1½ cups (150 g) of the pecans. Spread the mixture in a parchment paper–lined 8-inch (20 cm) square pan and freeze for 12 hours. Chop the praline into small chunks.

Chop remaining ¼ cup (25 g) pecans. Fold the pecans and 2 cups of the chopped praline, or more as desired (reserving the rest for another use), into the churned ice cream before freezing it for a few hours.

Yield 6 servings

triple berry ice cream

This recipe works as a great base for any berry ice cream. You could use as many or as few types of berries as desired. Cherries would be a nice addition, too.

Blend all but the coconut oil in a blender until completely smooth. Add the coconut oil and blend to incorporate. Chill the mixture in the fridge for 8 to 12 hours. Process it in an ice cream maker according to the manufacturer's instructions. Transfer the ice cream to a container and freezer for 5 to 6 hours.

Yield 4 servings

TIP You can add regular water in place of coconut water, but if you do, add extra coconut nectar to taste, as the coconut water is very sweet.

1 cup (145 g) blueberries

1 cup (125 g) raspberries

1 cup (170 g) diced strawberries

1 cup (137 g) cashews

¾ cup (175 ml) fresh coconut water

1½ tablespoons (22 ml) lemon juice

¼ cup + 1 tablespoon (105 g) agave or coconut nectar

1 teaspoon vanilla extract

2 tablespoons (30 ml) melted coconut oil

mint chip ice cream

I love to grow fresh mint in my herb garden in the summer, and this is one of my favorite uses for it. You can substitute cacao nibs for the chocolate chunks, but if you do, be sure to add a little more coconut nectar to the ice cream to compensate for their bitterness.

1½ cups (355 ml) water

1½ cups (205 g) cashews

¾ cup (72 g) lightly packed mint leaves

⅓ cup (115 g) coconut nectar

¾ teaspoon vanilla extract

3 tablespoons (45 ml) melted coconut oil

3 to 5 drops peppermint essential oil

1 cup (175 g) dark chocolate chunks (page 94)

Blend the water, cashews, mint, coconut nectar, and vanilla in a blender until smooth. Add the coconut oil and peppermint. Blend to combine. Chill the liquid mixture in the fridge for at least 8 hours and then process it in an ice cream maker according to the manufacturer's instructions. Toward the end of churning, add the chocolate chunks. Transfer the ice cream to a container and freeze for a few hours until it firms up more.

Yield 6 servings

pear sorbet

This one-ingredient sorbet is so creamy and sweet that you won't know there's no sweetener added to it. It's really easy to make and you don't have to peel the pears.

Process the pear chunks in a food processor until smooth and creamy. Serve immediately. Alternatively, process the pears in a high-speed blender until creamy using the tamper.

4 or 5 pears, cored, diced and frozen

Yield 1 or 2 servings

chocolate chip cookie dough ice cream cake

This cake is a party stopper and I'm certain you'll convert even the biggest raw food skeptics after they taste it. I like to decorate the top with extra cookie dough balls.

For the cake

1 batch chocolate chip cookie dough, without the chocolate chunks, before chilling (page 63)

1 cup (175 g) dark chocolate chunks (page 94)

2½ cups (350 g) freshly churned vanilla bean ice cream (page 74)

For the ganache

½ cup (161 g) maple syrup

⅓ cup (80 ml) melted coconut oil

⅔ cup (57 g) cacao powder

½ to 1 batch chocolate chip cookies, (page 63) for garnish, optional

To make the cake Press half of the cookie dough into the bottom of a 7-inch (18 cm) springform pan. Set aside. Fold the dark chocolate chunks into the freshly churned ice cream and spread it evenly over the cookie dough. Place the cake in the freezer until the ice cream is hard and then press the remaining cookie dough on top. Leave the cake out for about 20 minutes, or until the sides soften just enough that you can slide a knife between the cake and the pan to remove the ring. Place the cake back in the freezer while making the ganache.

To make the ganache Add the ingredients to a blender in the order given. Blend on low speed, and then on high until completely smooth and slightly warm from blending. Pour the ganache over the top of the cake and use an offset spatula to evenly and quickly spread it over the top and sides before it firms up on the cold cake.

Optional: Make a half or full batch of chocolate chip cookies and press them into the top of the cake. Freeze the cake for at least 30 minutes before slicing it.

Yield 12 servings

chocolate-covered strawberry chai ice cream

Chai spices, strawberries, and cashews get swirled together into a rich and creamy ice cream that gets dipped into dark chocolate. It's a grown-up version of the ice cream on a stick that I enjoyed as a child!

2½ cups (362 g) hulled, diced, packed strawberries

1½ cups (205 g) cashews

½ cup (170 g) agave or coconut nectar

2½ teaspoons (6 g) cinnamon

2½ teaspoons (6 g) cardamom

1½ teaspoons ground ginger

1 teaspoon ground cloves

½ teaspoon black pepper

½ teaspoon freshly grated nutmeg

½ teaspoon allspice

2 tablespoons (30 ml) melted coconut oil

1 batch, approximately 2½ cups (700 g) basic dark chocolate (page 94)

Blend all the ingredients except for the coconut oil in a blender until completely smooth. Add the oil and blend again to incorporate. Chill the liquid in the fridge for 8 to 12 hours.

The mixture will thicken a lot. Process it in an ice cream machine according to the manufacturer's instructions and then quickly spread it into a parchment paper–lined 8-inch (20 cm) square pan. Freeze it for 5 to 6 hours, or until it is firm enough to cut into with a 1- to 1½-inch (2.5 to 3.5 cm) round cookie cutter or cut it into squares with a knife. Cut the scraps into small pieces. Dip both the rounds and the scraps into the melted dark chocolate. (see page 97).

Yield 6 to 8 servings

carob-cinnamon ripple ice cream

Even if you don't like carob, I encourage you to give this recipe a try. Everyone I've served this ice cream to, carob lovers or not, really enjoys it. Add more cinnamon for a stronger taste.

2 cups (475 ml) water

1¾ cups (240 g) cashews

⅓ cup + 3 tablespoons (167 g) maple syrup

2 tablespoons (14 g) cinnamon

1 teaspoon vanilla extract

2 tablespoons (30 ml) melted coconut oil

¼ cup + 1 tablespoon (32 g) carob powder

Blend the water, cashews, maple syrup, cinnamon, and vanilla in a blender until completely smooth. Add the coconut oil. Blend again to incorporate. Pour all but 1 cup (235 ml) of the liquid into a bowl. Add the carob to the reserved liquid in the blender and blend to incorporate. Chill both liquids in the fridge for at least 12 hours. Process the cinnamon liquid in an ice cream machine according to the manufacturer's instructions. Spread one-third of the cinnamon ice cream into a container with a flat bottom, approximately 4 to 5 x 6 inches (10 to 13 x 15 cm). Pour half of the carob cream on top. Spread another one-third of the ice cream over the top followed by the rest of the carob cream. Spread the remaining ice cream on top. Work quickly as the ice cream will start melting quickly. Transfer to the freezer for at least 5 hours or until the ice cream firms up.

Yield 4 to 6 servings

chapter seven | **chocolate**

Chocolate is one of my favorite foods, and I eat it every day, but I eat organic raw chocolate that I make myself. Chocolate has a bad reputation but that's only because it's heavily processed with unhealthy ingredients like white sugar and milk. Raw cacao is completely different. It contains a lot of nutrients and is high in antioxidants. Now you can make your own healthy raw chocolate and feel good about eating it.

basic dark chocolate

Here's a basic chocolate recipe to be used for all my recipes that call for melted dark chocolate or dark chocolate chunks. This recipe is perfect for dipping whatever your heart desires. I love chocolate-dipped cherries, bananas, and dried jackfruit. I add nuts and dried fruits to extra melted chocolate to make clusters.

About 1½ cups (175 g) finely chopped cacao butter

¾ cup (241 g) maple syrup, or (255 g) agave or coconut nectar

1½ cups (129 g) cacao powder

to make
chocolate chunks

I like to use leftover melted chocolate to make chunks. They make great toppings for ice cream and are used in my chocolate chip cookie recipe.

Pour some melted chocolate into a parchment paper-lined container. Use any size container to accommodate the amount of chocolate you are using, making the chocolate as thick or thin as you like. Transfer the container to the fridge for 20 to 60 minutes or until firm. Chop it into chunks and store it at room temperature or in the fridge.

To make the chocolate After chopping the cacao butter, place it into a large glass or metal bowl over a pot with a bit of water in it. (Make sure the bottom of the bowl does not touch the water.) Heat the pot on the stove over low heat, allowing the butter to melt very slowly. Turn the heat on and off periodically. Keeping the heat very low will still ensure a raw product. You can touch the bottom of the bowl to make sure it's not too hot or stick your finger in the cacao butter. It will take a while to melt. Keep checking on it.

Once the butter has melted, measure 1 cup (235 ml). Pour any excess into a separate container for later use. Pour the cup (235 ml) of butter back into the bowl over the pot of hot water. Gently and briefly whisk in the maple syrup or nectar. Make sure your heat is still on low. Sift in the cacao powder. (Sifting is important or the chocolate will be lumpy.) Gently whisk the cacao powder into the liquid until it's incorporated and the mixture is smooth. Whisk a lot to evenly distribute the cacao butter. If it becomes difficult to stir in the cacao and the mixture is becoming stiff, turn the heat up slightly. Adding the sweetener and cacao powder will lower the temperature of the butter, so you may need to compensate with a bit of extra heat temporarily. But if you keep it on the heat too long, the chocolate will lose its proper consistency and separate. Once the mixture is smooth, turn off the heat and keep the bowl over the pot of hot water. The chocolate is now ready for using. Periodically touch the chocolate (or taste it or dab a bit just above your top lip). If it becomes warm to the touch, remove the bowl from the pot of hot water for a while.

Yield About 2½ cups (700 g) melted chocolate

how to **make dark chocolate**

You only need time and the proper ingredients to make raw, dark chocolate.

1

2

3

4

5

6

1. Chop cacao butter into small chunks on a clean and dry cutting board.

2. Slowly melt the cacao butter in a bowl that is sitting over a pot of hot water on the stove. Keep the heat on very low.

3. Measure the cacao butter after it's melted. Melt more or pour any extra into a separate container for next time.

4. Slowly whisk in the sweetener and cacao powder.

5. The chocolate is ready when it's completely smooth.

6. Finished chocolate will be very fluid and stream off the whisk.

white chocolate vanilla bean truffles

These decadent and delicious truffles have long been a part of my chocolate repertoire. They're always a hit—especially at the holidays—and I'm happy to pass the recipe along so that you can make them, too! For an added boost of vanilla flavor, add 5 or 6 drops vanilla medicine flower essence.

1 cup (137 g) cashews

¼ cup (80 g) maple syrup or (85 g) agave nectar

¼ cup (60 ml) warm water

½ teaspoon vanilla extract

Seeds of ½ to 1 vanilla bean

2 pinches Himalayan salt

¼ cup (60 ml) melted cacao butter (page 23)

2 or 3 drops stevia, optional

1 batch, approximately 2½ cups (700 g) basic dark chocolate (page 94)

¼ cup (36 g) lucuma

Blend the cashews, maple syrup or agave, water, and vanilla extract in a blender until smooth. Add the vanilla bean seeds, salt, and cacao butter. Blend to incorporate. Add a few drops of stevia if needed. It should be sweet enough to contrast with the dark chocolate it will be covered with. Pour the mixture into a large flat container and chill in the fridge for 8 to 12 hours. Roll into ½-inch (1 cm) balls and chill in the freezer for at least 6 hours, or until firm. Transfer the balls to the fridge while making the dark chocolate. Dip the truffles into the basic dark chocolate, one at a time and use a fork to transfer them to a parchment paper–lined tray. Once the chocolate has dried, sift lucuma over the truffles.

Yield 22 truffles

TIP If your hands are too warm, they will melt the mixture when you try to roll it. Run your hands under cold water periodically if you need to.

how to **cover anything with chocolate**

Use this simple method to coat anything in chocolate—try cherries, bananas, and dried jackfruit.

1

2

3

1. Place the bar (or whatever else you want to dip) into a bowl of melted basic dark chocolate. Use a fork to push the bar down into the chocolate so that it is completely coated.

2. Use the fork to lift the bar out of the chocolate, allowing the excess to drip back into the bowl. Scrape the bottom of the fork on the edge of the bowl if there is still a lot of excess chocolate dripping.

3. Carefully transfer the bar onto a parchment paper–lined tray.

macaroon squares

These are for the chocolate and coconut lovers in your midst. They make a great snack and pack especially well for traveling.

1 cup (280 g) basic dark chocolate (page 94)

3 cups (240 g) shredded coconut

2/3 cup (60 g) chopped almonds

½ cup (75 g) raisins

¼ cup + 2 tablespoons (120 g) maple syrup

1 teaspoon vanilla extract

⅛ teaspoon Himalayan salt

Stir all ingredients together in a large bowl over a pot of hot water on the stove. Spread the mixture into a parchment paper–lined 8-inch (20 cm) square pan, or use a 9-inch (23 cm) square pan for thinner squares. Chill in the fridge for at least 4 hours. Slice into 1½-inch (3.5 cm) squares.

Yield 25 squares (*photo at right*)

TIP It's important to keep the mixing bowl over another bowl of hot water on the stove (on very low heat) while combing the ingredients or the chocolate will get cold and seize.

crispy crunchy chocolate bars

These chocolate bars are crunchy, sweet, and full of texture. The dates are optional but they add chewiness and sweetness that I love.

½ cup (140 g) basic dark chocolate (page 94)

2 tablespoons (18 g) coconut sugar

2 tablespoons (20 g) buckwheat crunchies (page 34)

1 to 2 tablespoons (7 to 14 g) chopped nuts

2 teaspoons (3 g) cacao nibs

2 dates, finely chopped and broken apart, optional

12 drops vanilla medicine flower extract

Stir all the ingredients together in a bowl sitting over a pot of hot water (making sure the water doesn't touch the bowl). Make sure the chocolate is warm enough to stay fluid. Spoon the chunky mixture into chocolate bar molds and use a mini offset spatula to spread it evenly. Place them in the fridge to firm up, up to 2 hours, or until the chocolate easily falls out of the molds after turning them over.

Yield 4 bars

chocolate-covered chewy toffee

What's better than sweet chewy toffee covered in dark chocolate? These delicious treats make a great Christmas present and are so much better for you than regular sugar-filled toffee.

½ cup (161 g) maple syrup or (170 g) agave nectar

⅓ cup + 1 tablespoon (59 g) coconut sugar, ground

⅓ cup (80 ml) melted coconut butter (page 32)

¼ cup (64 g) almond butter

⅓ cup + 1 tablespoon (95 ml) melted coconut oil

1 tablespoon vanilla extract

⅛ teaspoon Himalayan salt

1 batch, approximately 2½ cups (700 g) basic dark chocolate (page 94)

Stir together all the ingredients except the dark chocolate in a bowl that is sitting on a pot of hot water. Pour the mixture into a parchment paper-lined 8-inch (20 cm) square pan. Chill in the freezer for at least 12 hours. Transfer the toffee and parchment paper to a cutting board and cut into 1½-inch (3.5 cm) squares or cut 2-inch (5 cm) squares and halve the squares to make triangles. Separate the toffee pieces on the parchment paper so they are not touching. Re-freeze for at least 12 hours before dipping into chocolate.

Dip each piece of frozen toffee into the chocolate and lift it out with a fork. Let excess chocolate drip back into the bowl and then scrape the fork on the edge of the bowl before setting the chocolate on a parchment paper–lined tray. Set in the fridge until the chocolate hardens, 15 to 30 minutes.

Yield 32 triangles or 25 squares

white chocolate

This white chocolate tastes just like the real thing and has a nice snap to it. I've used xylitol as the sweetener to keep it white, but it also has the added bonus of having no impact on your blood sugar. Feel free to stir in cacao nibs, goji berries, or anything else you like before pouring the chocolate into the molds.

Combine all ingredients into a blender until completely smooth. Pour into small silicone molds and chill in the fridge for at least 1 hour, or until firm.

Yield 20 to 24 pieces

TIP It's important to avoid using any liquid in the recipe in order to keep the chocolate hard.

⅓ **cup (80 ml) melted cacao butter (page 23)**

⅓ **cup (80 ml) melted coconut butter (page 32)**

¼ **cup (50 g) powdered xylitol**

30 drops vanilla medicine flower essence

caramel peanut chocolate bars

If you're looking for a sweet afternoon energy boost, indulge in one of these bars! My friends are always amazed at how delicious a faux, healthy "Snickers" bar can be.

For the nougat

1½ cups (205 g) cashews

1 tablespoon (9 g) coconut sugar, finely ground

2 tablespoons (40 g) agave nectar

1½ tablespoons (37 ml) melted coconut oil

For the caramel

⅔ cup (120 g) packed dates

⅓ cup (115 g) agave nectar

2 teaspoons (10 ml) vanilla extract

⅛ teaspoon Himalayan salt

⅓ cup (80 ml) melted coconut oil

¾ to 1 cup (105 to 145 g) wild jungle peanuts

For assembly

1 batch, approximately 2½ cups (700 g) basic dark chocolate (page 94)

To make the nougat Grind the cashews and coconut sugar in a food processor. Add the agave and coconut oil. Blend briefly to incorporate. Press the dough into an 8-inch (20 cm) square pan.

To make the caramel Purée the dates in a food processor. Add the agave, vanilla, and salt, and process to incorporate. Add the oil and process again until evenly mixed. Transfer the caramel to a bowl and fold in the peanuts. Spread the mixture over the nougat. Chill in the freezer for 8 to 12 hours. Slice into approximate 1⅓ x 2-inch (3.3 x 5 cm) bars and re-freeze until ready to dip into chocolate.

To assemble Dip each bar into the melted chocolate. Pull it out with a fork, allowing excess chocolate to drip back into the bowl, then scrape the fork on the edge of the bowl. Set the bar on a parchment paper–lined tray and pull out the fork from underneath. Chill the bars in the fridge until the chocolate is hard, 15 to 30 minutes.

Yield 24 bars

chocolate hazelnut spread

Enjoy this rich nutty chocolate spread on bananas, strawberries, apple slices, or raw bread. Or use it to make a Chocolate Hazelnut Parfait (page 133).

Make sure the ingredients are at room temperature. Blend all but the coconut oil in a high-speed blender until very smooth. Add the oil and blend again to incorporate. Chill it in the fridge for at least 6 hours, or until it firms up slightly. Add a bit more milk if you prefer a slightly thinner spread. It will keep for 6 to 7 days.

Yield   1 cup (260 g)

½ cup (130 g) hazelnut butter (page 31)

¼ cup + 1 tablespoon (75 ml) hazelnut milk (page 30)

⅓ cup (50 g) coconut sugar

3 tablespoons (16 g) cacao powder

½ teaspoon vanilla extract

2 pinches Himalayan salt

2 tablespoons (30 ml) melted coconut oil

triple chocolate layer bars

In this recipe, a chocolate cream is layered between brownies and covered in a white chocolate lucuma coating. I recommend giving the bars a double coating of the white chocolate to make it thick.

For the dough

2 cups (290 g) almonds

⅔ cup (120 g) packed dates

¾ cup (110 g) raisins

1 teaspoon vanilla extract

1½ to 2 teaspoons (7 to 10 ml) water, or as needed

½ cup (50 g) pecans or (60 g) walnuts

½ cup (43 g) cacao powder

⅛ teaspoon Himalayan salt

For the filling

1⅓ cups (182 g) cashews

⅓ cup (80 ml) water

¼ cup + 1 tablespoon (105 g) agave or coconut nectar

2 teaspoons (10 ml) vanilla extract

5½ to 6 tablespoons (30 to 32 g) cacao powder

⅓ cup (80 ml) melted coconut oil

To make the dough Grind the almonds in a food processor. Transfer them to a bowl. Purée the dates, raisins, vanilla, and 1½ teaspoons (7 ml) water in the processor, periodically scraping the processor and breaking up the mixture if it lumps together. Add the almond mixture, pecans or walnuts, cacao powder, and salt. Process until all the ingredients are broken down. Add ½ teaspoon more water if needed for the dough to hold together. Press half of the dough into an 8-inch (20 cm) square pan. Set aside.

To make the filling Blend the cashews, water, nectar, and vanilla in a blender until smooth and creamy. Add the cacao powder and coconut oil. Blend to incorporate. Add more cacao powder if desired for a darker chocolate taste. Pour the filling over the chocolate brownie dough and spread evenly. Chill in the freezer for at least 8 hours, or until firm.

Once the chocolate filling is chilled, press the other half of the chocolate dough on top. Slice into 1½ x 2-inch (3.5 x 5 cm) bars, or if they are too hard let sit in the fridge or at room temperature until they can be sliced. Store in the freezer before dipping.

To make the white lucuma chocolate Grind the cashews in a food processor. Add all the ingredients including the cashews to a blender and blend until smooth and creamy. Transfer to a bowl and let sit for 30 to 40 minutes, stirring periodically. The mixture will be warm from the melted cacao butter and coconut butter and from being blended. As the mixture cools, it will thicken to allow for coating the bars.

To assemble Dunk a bar into the chocolate and carefully lift out with a fork, scraping excess chocolate on the edge of the bowl. Work quickly. The chocolate will start to harden. Transfer to a parchment paper–lined tray. Repeat with the remaining bars. Chill in the fridge for at least 30 minutes to allow the chocolate to harden. Optional: Give a second coat of chocolate to each bar. Chill again.

Yield 20 bars

TIP The naked bars can be stored in the freezer for up to one month before dipping them.

For the white lucuma chocolate

1⅓ cups (182 g) cashews

⅔ cup (160 ml) melted cacao butter (page 23)

½ cup + 2 tablespoons (92 g) lucuma

½ cup (120 ml) melted coconut butter (page 32)

¼ cup (38 g) coconut sugar

10 drops stevia

30 drops vanilla medicine flower essence

chocolate peanut butter fudge

We all know that chocolate and peanut butter go together. It's been a longtime favorite combination of mine. The wild jungle peanut flavor really shines through in this fudge, adding a very raw, slightly bitter taste.

⅔ cup (187 g) basic dark chocolate (page 94)

⅔ cup (164 g) raw jungle peanut butter (page 31)

⅓ cup + 2 tablespoons (147 g) maple syrup

1½ teaspoons vanilla extract

⅛ teaspoon Himalayan salt

¼ cup (35 g) jungle peanuts, chopped, plus more for sprinkling

Stir all the ingredients except the peanuts together in a bowl that is sitting over a bowl of hot water on the stove in order to keep the mixture warm (to prevent the chocolate from seizing). Stir in the peanuts. Spread the fudge into a parchment paper–lined 8-inch (20 cm) square pan and sprinkle extra peanuts on top, if desired. Chill in the fridge for at least 2 hours. Slice into 1½-inch (3.5 cm) squares.

Yield 25 pieces

TIP You can try this with other nut butters, but because the peanut butter is slightly bitter than most, you will have to decrease the maple syrup slightly, to taste.

milk chocolate

It took me a number of trials to get this recipe just right. It was worth it. I haven't had store-bought milk chocolate in years, but I think this could rival the real thing.

Blend all ingredients in a high-speed blender until smooth. Pour into small silicone chocolate molds or chocolate bar molds. Chill in the fridge for at least 2 hours.

Yield 28 to 30 small pieces

TIP The vanilla medicine flower extract adds necessary flavor. Do not add any vanilla extract or any liquid or the chocolate will be slightly soft instead of hard and stable.

⅓ cup + ½ tablespoon (87 ml) melted cacao butter (page 23)

⅓ cup + ½ tablespoon (87 ml) melted coconut butter (page 32)

⅓ cup (45 g) cashews

2 tablespoons + 2 (teaspoons (14 g) cacao powder

2½ tablespoons (11 g) powdered xylitol

9 drops vanilla medicine flower extract

chocolate almond truffles

These chocolate truffles are really easy to make. I like to dress them up by rolling them in extra cacao powder, dipping them in dark chocolate (see page 97), or sprinkling chopped almonds on top.

1 cup (145 g) almonds

1½ cups (267 g) packed dates, chopped

¼ cup + 2 tablespoons (32 g) cacao powder

2 pinches Himalayan salt

2½ tablespoons (37 ml) melted cacao butter (page 23)

½ teaspoon vanilla extract

1½ teaspoons almond extract

Grind the almonds into flour in a food processor. Add the dates, cacao powder, and salt. Process until the mixture is completely broken down and smooth. Add the cacao butter, vanilla, and almond extract, and process again. The batter will be slightly sticky. Chill in the fridge for 2 to 4 hours and then roll it into ¾-inch (1.8 cm) balls.

Yield 26 truffles

chocolate caramel cups

Bite into hard dark chocolate filled with gooey caramel for a moment of bliss. I like to top mine with mulberries, chopped cashews, or coconut flakes.

When making the caramel recipe, add 1 additional tablespoon (9 g) lucuma and chill for at least 8 hours.

Spread a spoonful of melted chocolate into the bottom and sides of a mini silicone muffin cup. Transfer it to the freezer while moving on to the next cup. When you put the second cup into the freezer, take the first one out and place it on a baking sheet or plate. The chocolate should have hardened. Spread a second layer of chocolate in the each cup, focusing on the sides. (Leave ¼ to ⅓ cup [70 to 93 g] chocolate for the tops.) Set it in the freezer again and repeat with remaining cups. Once the chocolate is firm, spoon some of the caramel into each cup, leaving room for chocolate on top. Pour a small spoonful of chocolate on top and spread it using a mini offset spatula. Sprinkle mulberries or chopped nuts on top, if desired, before the chocolate sets. Chill in the fridge for at least 30 minutes before eating.

Yield 12 to 14 mini cups

1 batch, approximately 1 cup (240 g) caramel sauce (page 33)

1 tablespoon (9 g) lucuma

½ batch, approximately 1¼ cups (350g) basic dark chocolate (page 94)

Mulberries, for garnish, optional

Chopped nuts, for garnish, optional

mint chocolate swirl bark

Refreshing peppermint-infused white chocolate and rich dark chocolate are swirled together into pieces of bark that burst with flavor. Feel free to add enough spirulina to give a stronger green color.

1 batch, about ⅔ cup (160 g) melted white chocolate (page 101, before chilling)

8 to 12 drops peppermint essential oil

⅛ teaspoon spirulina, optional

¾ cup (210 g) basic dark chocolate (page 94)

Combine the melted white chocolate with the peppermint oil and spirulina in a blender and blend briefly to incorporate. Taste and add more peppermint oil as desired. When both chocolates are prepared (make sure the dark chocolate is warm and runny), pour ½ cup (120 g) of the melted white chocolate into a parchment paper–lined 8-inch (20 cm) square pan and tilt it to spread the chocolate around. It doesn't have to be perfect. Pour ⅔ cup (177 g) of the melted dark chocolate over the top in blobs and then spoon the remaining melted white chocolate in blobs over the top. Swirl the two chocolates together using a chopstick. Spoon the rest of the dark chocolate in blobs on top and swirl it in with the chopstick. Work quickly before the chocolate starts to firm up. Set the pan in the fridge for at least 2 hours, or until it is hard. Break it into approximately 2-inch (5 cm) pieces, by hand.

Yield 10 to 12 pieces

TIP Make the white chocolate while the cacao butter is melting for the dark chocolate.

chapter eight | **pies and tarts**

Guilt-free pies and tarts? Yes, please! Say goodbye to flour crusts and sugary fillings, and say hello to nut crusts and fresh fruit fillings. You'll find something for for every taste and season in this chapter, from chocolate to berries, tropical flavors, pumpkin, caramel apples, and more.

Serve up Lemon-Ginger Blackberry Pie, page 122.

piña colada pie

This is one of my favorite tropical drinks turned into dessert form. The filling is light and almost fluffy, with juicy chunks of pineapple throughout. Garnish with coconut flakes and diced pineapple if desired.

For the crust

1 cup (80 g) shredded coconut

¾ cup (107 g) almonds

⅔ cup (100 g) raisins

2 teaspoons (10 ml) water

2 pinches Himalayan salt

For the filling

2⅓ cups (365 g) diced pineapple, divided

½ cup (approximately 85 g) well-packed young coconut pulp

¼ cup (34 g) cashews

3 tablespoons (60 g) agave or coconut nectar

¼ teaspoon vanilla extract

Pinch Himalayan salt

¼ cup + 2 tablespoons (90 ml) melted coconut oil

2 tablespoons (30 ml) melted coconut butter (page 32)

1 cup (200 g) coconut whipped cream (page 34)

To make the crust Grind the coconut and almonds in a food processor until broken down to meal. Add the raisins and grind until they are completely broken down. Add the water and the salt and process briefly. The dough should be moist enough to hold together but not sticky. Press the dough into the bottom and sides of a 9-inch (23 cm) pie plate. Set aside.

To make the filling Blend 1 cup (165 g) of the diced pineapple, coconut pulp, cashews, nectar, vanilla, and salt until smooth in a blender. Add the oil and butter. Blend to incorporate. Transfer the filling to a bowl. Fold in the remaining 1⅓ cups (250 g) diced pineapple. Spoon the filling into the crust. Chill it in the fridge for at least 12 hours. Spread coconut whipped cream over the pie filling.

Yield 12 servings

chocolate fudge tart

I created this tart at the request of a customer, and I'm so glad I did. It's decadent, silky, and perfect for a chocolate lover! To make it even richer, spread a thin layer of chocolate sauce (page 32) on the crust before adding the filling and drizzle chocolate sauce on top before serving the tart.

To make the crust Grind the almonds, sunflower seeds, and coconut in a food processor until finely ground. Add the raisins, dates, and cacao powder. Process until completely broken down. Add the salt, vanilla and 1½ teaspoons (7 ml) of the water and process until incorporated. If the dough isn't holding together easily when pressed in your hand, add the remaining ½ teaspoon of water. Press the dough evenly into an 8-inch (20 cm) tart pan with a removable bottom. Set aside.

To make the filling Combine all ingredients in a food processor adding the water last so that it stays hot. Process the mixture until it comes thick and smooth, 15 to 30 seconds. Spread the filling into the crust. Chill in the fridge for at least 8 hours before slicing.

Yield 12 servings

For the crust

¾ cup (107 g) almonds

¼ cup (35 g) sunflower seeds

¼ cup (20 g) shredded coconut

½ cup (75 g) raisins

¼ cup (45 g) dates

¼ cup (22 g) cacao powder

⅛ teaspoon Himalayan salt

½ teaspoon vanilla extract

1½ to 2 teaspoons (7 to 10 ml) water

For the filling

⅓ cup + 1 tablespoon (102 g) almond butter

⅓ cup + 2 tablespoons (147 g) maple syrup

Scant ½ cup (43 g) cacao powder

½ teaspoon vanilla extract

⅓ cup (80 ml) melted coconut oil

1 to 2 teaspoons (5 to 10 ml) hot water

pumpkin pie

This raw version of a classic holiday pie has no pumpkin in it! Raw sweet potato is used in the filling instead, but you'd never guess it. The candied pumpkin seeds add a nice touch.

For the crust

1 cup (145 g) almonds

⅔ cup (87 g) pumpkin seeds

½ cup (40 g) shredded coconut

½ cup (89 g) packed dates

Pinch Himalayan salt

2 to 3 teaspoons (10 to 15 ml) water

For the pumpkin seeds

¼ cup (16 g) pumpkin seeds

1 tablespoon (20 g) maple syrup

2 teaspoons (6 g) coconut sugar

1 teaspoon melted coconut oil

For the filling

3 cups (330 g) peeled, grated, packed sweet potato

1 cup (137 g) cashews

6 large dates

¼ cup (80 g) maple syrup

1 tablespoon (6 g) grated ginger

1 tablespoon + 1 teaspoon (9 g) cinnamon

1½ teaspoons vanilla extract

1 teaspoon fresh grated nutmeg

½ teaspoon ground cloves

½ teaspoon ground allspice

⅛ teaspoon Himalayan salt

¼ cup + 3 tablespoons (105 ml) melted coconut oil

1 cup (200 g) coconut whipped cream (page 34)

To make the crust Grind the almonds, seeds, and coconut into meal in a food processor. Add the dates and salt. Process until completely broken down. Add 2 teaspoons (10 ml) of the water and process briefly. If the mixture is slightly moist and holds together when pressed in your hand, it's finished. If not, add the remaining 1 teaspoon (5 ml) water and process briefly to incorporate it. Press the dough into a 9-inch (23 cm) pie plate. Set aside.

To make the pumpkin seeds Toss together all ingredients. Spread on a parchment paper–lined plate and chill in the freezer for at least 1 hour. (They will be sticky.)

To make the filling Blend all but the coconut oil and whipped cream in a blender until completely smooth and creamy. Add the oil and blend to incorporate. Spread the filling into the pie crust. Chill in the fridge for 12 hours. Top with coconut whipped cream, and arrange the candied pumpkin seeds around the edge of the chilled pie.

Yield 12 servings

almond pear cream tart

In this tart, a delicious dried pear crust is filled with blackberry jam, almond cream, and fresh pears. It's a perfect dessert for any time of year.

To make the crust Grind the almonds, coconut, and dried pear in a food processor. Add the dates and water. Grind until the dates are incorporated. Press the dough into an 8-inch (20 cm) tart pan with a removable bottom. Spread the jam over the tart crust. Chill in the freezer while making the filling.

To make the filling Blend the cashews, water, nectar, and extracts in a blender until smooth and creamy. Add the butter, oil, and stevia. Blend again to incorporate. Pour the filling over the jam. Chill in the freezer for 4 to 6 hours and then in the fridge for 8 to 12 hours. Pop the whole tart out of the pan.

To assemble Once the filling is firm, arrange the pear slices on the top of the tart. Slice and serve.

Yield 12 servings

For the crust
1 cup (145 g) almonds

⅔ cup (54 g) shredded coconut

¾ cup (97 g) finely chopped dried pear

⅓ cup (60 g) packed dates

1½ teaspoons water

⅓ cup (100 g) blackberry jam (page 33) or other berry jam

For the filling
½ cup (68 g) cashews

⅓ cup (80 ml) water

2 tablespoons (40 g) agave or coconut nectar

½ to ¾ teaspoon almond extract

½ teaspoon vanilla extract

¼ cup (60 ml) melted coconut butter (page 32)

1 tablespoon (15 ml) melted coconut oil

5 or 6 drops stevia

For assembly
1 or 2 pears, cored and thinly sliced

caramel apple turnovers

Apples and caramel get "baked" in an almond pastry crust in this dessert. They're best eaten warm out of the dehydrator.

For the filling

2⅔ cups (375 g) peeled, diced apples

½ cup (120 g) caramel sauce (page 33)

⅓ cup (33 g) chopped pecans, optional

For the dough

1⅓ cups (188 g) almonds

½ cup (89 g) dates

¼ cup + 2 tablespoons (42 g) ground flax

1 teaspoon cinnamon

1 tablespoon + 2 teaspoons (25 ml) water

To make the filling Toss the diced apples and caramel sauce. Spread on a ParaFlexx-lined dehydrator tray. Dehydrate at 145°F (63°C) for 1 hour and then at 115°F (46°C) for 5 to 6 hours. Fold in the pecans, if using.

To make the dough Grind the almonds into flour in a food processor. Add the dates, flax, and cinnamon. Grind again until evenly combined. Add the water and process briefly into a pliable dough. The dough needs to be moist enough to roll without cracking. Roll the dough between 2 large pieces of parchment paper to barely ¼-inch (6 mm) thick. Cut the dough into 3-inch (7.5 cm) squares and transfer each piece to a dehydrator tray. Continue rolling and cutting the dough scraps until all the dough is used. You should have 8 squares.

To assemble Arrange a few spoonfuls of apple filling on half of each piece of dough, forming a triangle of filling. Fold the dough over from corner to corner and use your fingers to press the dough together to seal it. Use a fork to gently crimp the edges. Dehydrate the turnovers on a mesh tray at 145°F (63°C) for 1 hour and then at 115°F (46°C) for 26 to 28 hours. Store in the fridge and eat within 3 days.

Yield 8 turnovers

spiced pear crumble

This lovely crumble combines fresh pears and spices with a dried mulberry and walnut topping. It can be warmed in the dehydrator before serving and goes perfectly with a scoop of Vanilla Bean Ice Cream (page 74).

To make the crumble Grind all but the water in a food process until broken down, leaving a bit of texture. Add the water and pulse to combine. Set aside.

To make the filling Whisk together the maple syrup, cinnamon, ginger, and cardamom in a small bowl. Add the diced pears to a bowl and pour the maple sauce over the top. Stir to evenly combine the sauce and pears. Use immediately or chill the mixture in the fridge to marinate for at 6 hours to allow the flavors to develop and the pears to soften. Transfer ½ cup (161 g) of the mixture to a separate bowl and mash it with a fork. Stir it back into the marinated pears and spread the mixture into an 8-inch (20 cm) square pan. Sprinkle the crumble over the top. Serve immediately.

Yield 6 or 7 servings

For the crumble

1½ cups (150 g) walnuts

1 cup (122 g) dried mulberries

3 large dates

2 pinches Himalayan salt

¾ teaspoon water

For the filling

3½ tablespoons (117 g) maple syrup

2½ teaspoons (5.75 g) cinnamon

¾ teaspoon ground ginger

¼ to ½ teaspoon ground cardamom

7 cups (1 kg + 50 g) diced pears

mango lime tarts

You could turn anyone into an avocado lover with these tropical tarts. They're a raw version of a cooked vegan dessert I had in Australia a few years ago.

For the crust

1½ cups + 2 tablespoons (130 g) shredded coconut

1⅓ cups (182 g) cashews or macadamia nuts

¼ cup + 2 tablespoons (65 g) buckwheat crunchies (page 34)

½ cup (89 g) packed dates

1 tablespoon + 1 teaspoon (20 ml) water

For the cream

¾ cup (131 g) diced, packed mango

¼ cup (34 g) mashed avocado

3 tablespoons (45 ml) lime juice

2 tablespoons (40 g) coconut nectar

½ teaspoon packed lime zest

¼ cup (60 ml) melted coconut oil

Chopped mango and kiwi, for garnish

To make the crust Finely grind the coconut, cashews, and buckwheat crunchies in a food processor. Add the dates. Process until they are broken down. Add the water and pulse to combine. Press the crust into four 4-inch (10 cm) tart shells. Set aside.

To make the cream Blend the mango, avocado, lime juice, nectar, and zest until smooth. Add the coconut oil and blend again to incorporate. Spread the cream into the crusts. Chill in the fridge for at least 6 hours. Garnish with the chopped mango and kiwi.

Yield 4 tarts

lemon-ginger blackberry pie

This gorgeous pink pie combines the tanginess of lemon with zingy ginger, sweet cashew cream, and juicy berries. You can make it with any berry, but only the frozen ones will bleed color into the filling to create an artistic swirl.

For the crust

1 cup (145 g) almonds

½ cup (40 g) shredded coconut

⅔ cup (86 g) packed dried apricots, chopped

¼ cup (45 g) dates

1 teaspoon water

For the filling

¾ cup (175 ml) lemon juice

1⅓ cups (182 g) cashews

⅓ cup + 2 tablespoons (145 g) agave or coconut nectar

1½ tablespoons (9 g) minced ginger (on a microplane)

1 teaspoon lemon zest

⅓ cup (80 ml) melted coconut oil

1 cup (145 g) fresh or (155 g) frozen blackberries

To make the crust Grind the almonds and coconut into flour in a food processor. Add the apricots and dates and process until they are completely broken down. This may take a little while if the apricots are firm. Add the water and pulse to combine. Press the crust into a 9-inch (23 cm) pie plate. Set aside.

To make the filling Blend the lemon juice, cashews, nectar, and ginger in a high-speed blender until smooth. Add the zest and coconut oil. Blend again to incorporate. Transfer the mixture to a bowl and fold in the blackberries. If using frozen berries, fold them in quickly so they don't clump together and start firming up the filling before you have a chance to spread it. Do not overmix if you want a colorful swirl in the filling. Evenly spread the filling into the crust. Chill in the freezer for 6 hours and then in the fridge for at least 8 hours.

Yield 12 servings

mint chocolate tartlets

These little tarts are the perfect finger food treat for a party. I like to dress them up with a drizzle of raw chocolate sauce (page 32) and fresh mint leaves.

To make the crust Grind the almonds into flour in a food processor. Add the raisins, dates, and cacao. Process until they are broken down. Add the water and pulse to combine. Press the dough into the bottom and sides of a plastic wrap–lined mini muffin tray with 12 muffin molds.

To make the filling Blend the cashews, water, syrup, and vanilla in a blender until smooth and creamy. Add the remaining ingredients and blend until you can only see specks of mint. Add more peppermint oil if desired. Pour the filling into the crusts. Chill in the fridge for at least 12 hours.

Yield 12 tartlets

For the crust

Scant 1cup (145 g) almonds

½ cup (75 g) raisins

½ cup (89 g) dates

2½ tablespoons (13 g) cacao powder

1 teaspoon water

For the filling

⅔ cup (90 g) cashews

¼ cup (60 ml) water

3 tablespoons (60 ml) maple syrup

¼ teaspoon vanilla extract

¼ cup (24 g) lightly packed mint leaves

1 tablespoon (15 ml) melted cacao butter (page 23)

1 tablespoon (15 ml) melted coconut oil

3 drops peppermint essential oil

chocolate raspberry marble pie

Chocolate, vanilla, and raspberries go together so well. I like to make this pie in the summer after picking raspberries in my backyard.

For the crust

¾ cup (109 g) sunflower seeds

1 cup (145 g) raisins

¼ cup (45 g) dates

⅔ cup (63 g) walnuts

3½ tablespoons (19 g) cacao powder

½ teaspoon vanilla extract

2 pinches Himalayan salt

For the filling

1½ cups (205 g) cashews

½ cup + 1 tablespoon (135 ml) water

⅓ cup + 1 tablespoon (135 g) agave nectar, divided

1 teaspoon vanilla extract

⅓ cup (80 ml) melted coconut oil

2 tablespoons (30 ml) melted cacao butter (page 23)

2 cups (250 g) raspberries

3 tablespoons (16 g) cacao powder

To make the crust Grind the sunflower seeds into flour in a food processor. Add the raisins and dates. Process until they are broken down. Add the walnuts, cacao, vanilla, and salt. Process again until the walnuts are broken down. Press the dough into a 9-inch (23 cm) pie plate. Set aside.

To make the filling Blend the cashews, water, ⅓ cup (115 g) of the agave, and vanilla until completely smooth. Add the coconut oil and cacao butter and blend again to incorporate. Transfer 1 heaping cup (240 g) of the mixture to a bowl and fold in the raspberries. Add the cacao powder and remaining 1 tablespoon (20 g) agave to the remaining mixture in the blender and blend to combine. Spread a thin layer of the chocolate mixture over the crust and pour the vanilla-raspberry mixture over the top. Pour large blobs of the chocolate mixture on top and use a chopstick to swirl the 2 mixtures together, creating a marble effect. Chill in the fridge for 12 to 16 hours.

Yield 12 servings

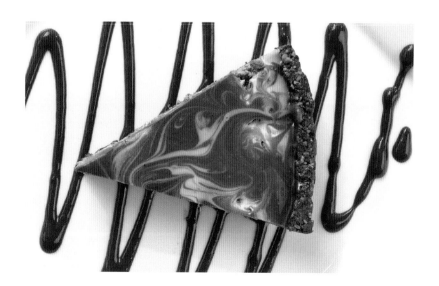

blueberry tart

I based this tart on the incredible blueberry pies my mom used to make after summertime blueberry picking in the forest near our house. It is simple but extremely delicious. There is a bit more crust than needed, so enjoy a "chef's sample."

To make the crust Grind the nuts, coconut, and flax seed into powder in a food processor. Add the dates and process until they are broken down. Pulse in the water. Press the crust into the bottom and sides of an 8-inch (20 cm) tart pan. Set aside.

To make the filling Blend 1⅔ cups (237 g) of the blueberries and remaining ingredients until smooth. Transfer the mixture to a bowl and fold in the remaining 1⅓ cups (198 g) berries. Evenly spread the filling into the crust. Chill in the fridge for at least 8 hours before serving.

Yield 12 servings

For the crust

1 cup (133 g) Brazil nuts

¾ cup (60 g) shredded coconut

¼ cup (28 g) ground flax seed

⅔ cup (120 g) packed dates

1¼ teaspoons water

For the filling

3 cups (435 g) blueberries, divided

½ cup (89 g) dates

1½ tablespoons (25 ml) lemon juice

1 tablespoon (10 g) chia seed

½ teaspoon vanilla extract

caramel banana cream tarts

In this recipe, yummy caramel, chunks of banana, and whipped cream are layered in a banana-nut crust. It's absolutely delicious. Be sure to find whole, dried bananas—not banana chips which are actually deep-fried.

For the crust

1 cup (178 g) packed, dried bananas

⅔ cup (86 g) almonds

½ cup (50 g) walnuts

2 pinches Himalayan salt

2 teaspoons (10 ml) water

For the filling

½ cup (89 g) well-packed dates

2 tablespoons (40 g) agave or coconut nectar

3 tablespoons (48 g) almond or pecan butter

1 teaspoon vanilla extract

2 teaspoons (10 ml) water

3 tablespoons (45 ml) melted coconut oil

For assembly

1 batch, 1 cup (240 g) caramel sauce (page 33)

3 or 4 bananas, diced

1 batch, 1½ cups (300 g) coconut whipped cream (page 34)

To make the crust Chop the dried bananas into small pieces. Grind the almonds into flour in a food processor. Add the banana and process until it is finely ground. Add the walnuts, salt, and water. Process until the walnuts are broken down to crumbs. (If you process more than that, the dough will become oily.) Press it into four 4-inch (10 cm) tart pans with removable bottoms. Freeze the tart crusts while making the caramel filling.

To make the filling Process the dates until as smooth as possible in a food processor. Add the nectar, nut butter, vanilla, and water. Process until smooth. Add the coconut oil and process to incorporate it.

To assemble Spread a thick layer of caramel into the tart crusts. Arrange a layer of diced bananas over the caramel in the tart crusts. Fold more bananas into the whipped cream and spoon the mixture into the tart crusts, mounding it up slightly. Arrange more bananas on top if desired and drizzle caramel sauce over the top.

Yield 4 tarts

chapter nine |
puddings and parfaits

Parfaits are one of my favorite desserts to make for guests. I like how each parfait can be constructed to suit each person's tastes, simple or elaborate. Being a person who likes different textures, I enjoy the combination of creamy layers, crunchy bits, juicy fruit, and chewy brownie or cake bits all in one dessert. Puddings are another great way to satisfy a craving for something sweet and creamy. They're easy to make and only require a blender.

tropical parfait

When you can't travel to the tropics, let the tropics come to you! In this parfait, a smooth fruity pudding is layered with a crunchy tropical granola, coconut whipped cream, and tropical fruit. Sit back, enjoy dessert, and pretend you're at the beach.

For the pudding

1½ cups (265 g) diced mango or pineapple

½ cup (90 g) packed orange segments

½ cup (approximately 85 g) packed young coconut pulp

2 teaspoons (6 g) coconut sugar

3 or 4 drops stevia

¼ teaspoon vanilla extract

1 tablespoon (30 ml) melted coconut oil

For the tropical granola

½ cup (60 g) buckwheat groats

1 cup (80 g) shredded coconut

½ cup (107 g) macadamia nuts, roughly chopped

½ cup (68 g) cashews, roughly chopped

⅓ cup (28 g) coconut flakes

1 cup (155 g) diced pineapple or mango

2 or 3 kiwis, peeled and diced small

¼ cup + 1 tablespoon (100 g) agave or coconut nectar

1 tablespoon (6 g) orange zest

For assembly

Chopped tropical fruit, for garnish

1 cup (200 g) coconut whipped cream (page 34)

To make the pudding Blend all but the coconut oil in a blender until smooth. Add the oil and blend to incorporate. Chill the pudding in the fridge for at least 4 hours.

To make the granola Soak the buckwheat in enough water to cover plus an extra inch (2.5 cm), for 2 to 4 hours. Rinse the buckwheat very well, until the water runs clear. Toss all the ingredients together and then spread on 2 ParaFlexx-lined dehydrator trays. Dehydrate at 145°F (63°C) for 1 hour and then at 115°F (45°C) for 32 to 36 hours, or until dry. You will have about a cup of granola left over. Store it in the freezer to keep it fresh and crunchy.

To assemble Layer tropical fruit pudding with tropical granola, fresh fruit of your choice, and coconut whipped cream.

Yield 3 or 4 servings

TIP Add ¾ cup (133 g) chopped dried tropical fruit *after* dehydrating in place of the fresh pineapple or mango if you like.

how to **layer a parfait**

Follow my instructions or use your creativity to layer a pretty parfait.

1. Start by sprinkling some diced fruit into the bottom of a glass.

2. Spoon some pudding over the fruit using a small enough spoon that no pudding gets smeared on the inside of the glass.

3. Sprinkle another layer of fruit on top followed by a layer of granola. Use your fingers to arrange how you want it to look.

4. Spoon some whipped cream on top. Use the back of the spoon to spread it around.

5. Spoon another layer of pudding on top.

6. Top it with more granola, coconut flakes, and/or diced fruit.

basic vanilla chia pudding

Chia seeds are packed with nutrients, protein, and healthy fat, plus they're extremely high in fiber. This simple pudding is great for a snack before a workout because it's hydrating and contains long-lasting energy. Add to smoothies for extra nutrition and satiety.

⅔ to ¾ cup (150 to 175 ml) almond milk (page 30)

1 tablespoon (10 g) chia seeds

⅛ teaspoon vanilla bean powder or ¼ teaspoon vanilla extract, optional

Stevia or sweetener of your choice, optional

Pour the almond milk, chia, and vanilla (if using) into a lidded jar or container. Shake well. Let the mixture sit for at least 30 minutes, shaking periodically to prevent the chia from clumping together. Add the sweetener (if using). You can eat it immediately, but it's best after it sits for a few hours or overnight. The chia absorbs the milk and swells completely, giving it the consistency of tapioca pudding.

Yield 1 serving

TIP Make a berry pudding by blending ⅔ cup (160 ml) almond milk with ⅓ cup (50 g) berries, mixing with the chia seeds. Add a few drops of raspberry medicine flower extract to boost the berry flavor.

chocolate chia pudding

Here's a chocolate version of the basic vanilla chia pudding. The addition of dates and cacao make it a decadent treat that's still so full of nutrition that it can be eaten for breakfast!

1½ cups (355 ml) almond milk (page 30)

½ cup (89 g) lightly packed dates

1½ tablespoons (8 g) cacao powder

½ teaspoon vanilla extract

3½ tablespoons (35 g) chia seed

Blend the almond milk, dates, cacao, and vanilla in a blender until completely smooth. Pour the liquid into a bowl and whisk in the chia seeds. Let the mixture sit for at least 2 hours and up to 12 hours to allow the chia to swell. Stir again before eating.

Yield 2 or 3 servings

chocolate hazelnut parfait

This gorgeous parfait is perfect for the chocolate lover. It combines a smooth pudding made with chocolate hazelnut spread, along with crunchy chocolate nut granola and rich chocolate sauce. I'm happy to eat a bowl of this hazelnut pudding alone. It's that good.

To make the pudding Blend all ingredients in a blender until smooth. Add enough hazelnut extract for your taste. Chill in the fridge for at least 6 hours. Add more hazelnut milk if you prefer a thinner pudding.

To make the granola Make sure the hazelnuts and buckwheat are rinsed and drained very well. Toss all ingredients together in a bowl. Add an extra teaspoon of cacao powder if desired or more maple syrup for a sweeter granola. Spread the mixture on a ParaFlexx-lined dehydrator tray. Dehydrate for 1 hour at 145°F (63°C) and then at 115°F (45°C) for 24 to 26 hours, until dry and crunchy.

To assemble Layer the chocolate hazelnut pudding, granola, and chocolate sauce in glasses. Serve immediately.

Yield 4 or 5 servings

For the pudding

½ cup hazelnut milk (page 30)

1 batch (about 1 cup [260 g]) chocolate hazelnut spread (page 103)

¼ cup (64 g) hazelnut butter (page 31)

¼ cup (38 g) coconut sugar

¼ to ½ teaspoon hazelnut extract

For the granola

½ cup (67 g) hazelnuts, soaked 4 to 6 hours

¼ cup buckwheat groats, soaked 2 to 4 hours

1 tablespoon (5 g) cacao powder

¼ teaspoon vanilla extract

¼ to ½ teaspoon hazelnut extract

3 tablespoons (60 g) maple syrup

1½ tablespoons (17 g) cacao nibs

For assembly

⅔ cup (160 g) chocolate sauce (page 32)

raspberry pomegranate white chocolate parfait

When a pomegranate caught my eye at the store during the holiday season I knew I had to come up with something beautiful and festive using it. White chocolate, vanilla bean, pomegranate, and raspberry come together to create a luscious parfait to serve to your guests.

For the white chocolate pudding

1 cup (235 ml) water

⅔ cup (90 g) cashews

½ teaspoon vanilla extract

¼ cup (50 g) xylitol

2 tablespoons (30 ml) melted cacao butter (page 23)

2 tablespoons + 1 teaspoon (35 ml) melted coconut butter (page 32)

Seeds of 1½ vanilla beans

For the raspberry pomegranate pudding

1⅓ cups (166 g) raspberries

⅔ cup (160 ml) pomegranate juice

⅔ cup (90 g) cashews

2½ tablespoons (50 g) agave or coconut nectar

¼ cup (60 ml) melted coconut oil

For assembly

1½ cups fresh (190 g) raspberries or ½ cup (160 g) berry sauce (page 33)

To make the white chocolate pudding Blend the water, cashews, vanilla, and xylitol until smooth and creamy in a blender. Add the butters and vanilla bean seeds. Blend to incorporate. Pour the liquid into an 8-inch (20 cm) square pan and chill in the fridge for 12 hours.

To make the raspberry pomegranate pudding Blend the raspberries, pomegranate juice, cashews, and nectar in a blender until smooth. Add the oil and blend to incorporate. Chill the pudding in the fridge for 8 to 12 hours.

To assemble Layer the 2 puddings with fresh raspberries or berry sauce.

Yield 4 to 6 servings

TIP To make pomegranate juice, put the seeds of 2 pomegranates in a blender and then strain out the juice using a nut milk bag. Compost the pulp. Alternatively, put the seeds through a juicer.

blackberry strawberry pudding

This pudding is perfect in the summer when berries are out in abundance. I've used creamy young coconut to thicken it, making it a great option for people who can't eat nuts.

Blend all ingredients but the coconut oil in a blender until smooth. Add the oil and blend again to incorporate. Chill the pudding in the fridge for at least 4 hours before serving.

Yield 2 servings

¾ cup (109 g) blackberries

¾ cup (127 g) diced strawberries

¾ cup (approximately 127 g) packed young coconut pulp
1 tablespoon + 2 teaspoons (33 g) agave or coconut nectar

½ teaspoon lemon juice

¼ teaspoon vanilla extract

2 teaspoons (10 ml) melted coconut oil

carrot cake parfait

Moist carrot cake crumbles, cashew cream cheese frosting, and pineapple chunks are combined to create a beautiful and delicious parfait. This is a fun way to eat carrots!

For the crumbles

1½ cups (120 g) shredded coconut

1 cup (150 g) walnuts

⅔ cup (120 g) packed dates, chopped

1½ teaspoons cinnamon

1½ cups (165 g) shredded carrot

½ teaspoon vanilla extract

Pinch Himalayan salt

For the frosting

¾ cup (175 ml) water

2 cups (274 g) cashews

¼ cup + 2 tablespoons (120 g) maple syrup

2 tablespoons (30 ml) lemon juice

¾ teaspoon vanilla extract

3 tablespoons (45 ml) melted coconut oil

For assembly

2 cups (310 g) diced pineapple

To make the crumbles Grind the coconut, walnuts, dates, and cinnamon into crumbs in a food processor. Add the carrot, vanilla, and salt. Pulse several times to evenly incorporate. Chill in the fridge until assembling the parfaits.

To make the frosting Blend all ingredients but the coconut oil until completely smooth in a blender. Add the oil and blend to incorporate. Add more lemon juice if you want it tangier. Chill the mixture in the fridge for 8 to 12 hours.

To assemble Layer the carrot cake crumbles, cream cheese frosting, and pineapple in glasses or bowls. Serve immediately.

Yield 4 to 6 servings

how to **cut a pineapple**

A pineapple is ripe when it has developed a strong pineapple smell, has become heavy with water, has turned from green to yellowy orange, and is slightly soft when pressed with your fingers.

1. Turn the pineapple on its side on a cutting board and cut the top and bottom off.

2. Turn the pineapple right side up and use a sharp knife to cut the skin in long strips from top to bottom, working all the way around. Use a paring knife to remove the little dimples that are left behind, as needed.

3. Cut from top to bottom on each side of the core, making two big chunks. Cut the other two pieces away from the core, cutting top to bottom. The core can be juiced.

4. Place each large pineapple chunk on its flat side and cut it into chunks. Transfer the cut pineapple to a sealed container and store it in the fridge for up to five days or in the freezer for up to two months.

tiramisu parfait

Here all the elements of traditional tiramisu are layered in glasses, making this dessert a feast for the eyes and the appetite. You don't have to worry about making coffee and soaking the cookies in it. I've added coffee extract right into the moist cake.

For the cake

½ cup (40 g) shredded coconut

½ cup (125 g) lightly packed almond pulp (page 30)

¼ cup (45 g) well-packed dates, finely chopped

½ teaspoon vanilla extract

9 or 10 drops coffee medicine flower extract

½ to 1 teaspoon water

For the cream

⅔ cup (90 g) cashews

½ cup (120 ml) water

2½ tablespoons (50 g) coconut nectar

1½ teaspoons vanilla extract

¾ teaspoon lemon juice

2½ tablespoons (37 ml) melted coconut oil

2 tablespoons (30 ml) melted coconut butter (page 32)

2 pinches turmeric, for color

For assembly

1 cup (200 g) coconut whipped cream (page 34)

1 chunk, approximately 2 ounces (56 g), basic dark chocolate (page 94), grated on a microplane

2 teaspoons (4 g) cacao powder

To make the cake Grind the coconut into flour in a food processor. Add the remaining ingredients and process to incorporate. Transfer to a bowl and place in the fridge.

To make the cream Blend the cashews, water, nectar, vanilla, and lemon juice in a blender until smooth. Add the oil, butter, and enough turmeric to make it pale yellow. Blend to incorporate. Chill in the fridge for 12 hours.

To assemble Sprinkle or spread the cake into the bottom of 4 to 6 small clear glasses. Spread the cream on top followed by a layer of whipped cream. Sprinkle a layer of grated chocolate on top. Repeat all the layers a second time. Serve immediately or chill in the fridge for 6 to 12 hours to let the flavors develop even more. Dust with cacao powder before serving.

Yield 4 to 6 servings

apple cinnamon pudding

This pudding is a thick and creamy version of applesauce. I like to make it in the fall with freshly picked apples.

Blend all ingredients in a high-speed blender until completely smooth and creamy. Serve immediately.

Yield 1 or 2 servings

2 cups (320 g) diced, peeled apple

¼ cup (45 g) well-packed dates

2 tablespoons (32 g) almond butter

1½ teaspoons cinnamon

½ teaspoon vanilla extract

½ teaspoon lemon juice

citrus coconut yogurt

This tangy coconut yogurt is so light and refreshing. I enjoy it as a breakfast treat when I have an abundance of coconuts and I like to top it with tropical granola (page 130).

Combine all ingredients in a blender until smooth and creamy. Chill the yogurt for at least 4 hours before serving.

Yield 2 to 4 servings

⅔ cup (160 ml) lemon juice

⅓ cup (80 ml) orange juice

1 cup (approximately 170 g) packed young coconut pulp

3 tablespoons (60 g) coconut nectar

2 teaspoons (4 g) packed lemon zest

mint chocolate parfait

Invigorating peppermint-infused pudding is layered with rich chocolate avocado pudding in this parfait. I think that the fresh mint combined with the essential oil makes the perfect flavor.

For the mint pudding

½ cup (120 ml) fresh coconut water

½ cup (68 g) cashews

⅔ cup (approximately 113 g) packed young coconut pulp

½ cup (48 g) lightly packed mint leaves

3 tablespoons (60 g) agave or coconut nectar

½ teaspoon vanilla extract

3 tablespoons (45 ml) melted coconut oil

4 drops peppermint essential oil

For the chocolate pudding

¾ cup (150 g) mashed avocado

½ cup (120 ml) water

⅓ cup (60 g) packed dates

2½ to 3 tablespoons (50 to 60 g) maple syrup

¼ cup (22 g) cacao powder

½ teaspoon vanilla extract

Pinch Himalayan salt

For assembly

¼ cup (44 g) cacao nibs or ½ cup (120 g) chocolate sauce (page 32), for garnish

To make mint pudding Blend the coconut water and cashews until smooth in a blender. Add the coconut pulp, mint, nectar, and vanilla. Blend again until the mint is broken down, but do not overblend because it will ruin the flavor of the mint. Add the coconut oil and peppermint. Blend to incorporate. Chill for at least 4 hours.

To make the chocolate pudding Combine all ingredients in a blender until completely smooth. Chill at least 4 hours.

To assemble Layer the chilled puddings in glasses alone or with a layer or cacao nibs or chocolate sauce.

Yield 3 or 4 servings

strawberry lemonade parfait

The sweet and tangy lemon pudding in this parfait uses avocado as its secret "creamy" ingredient. It's lemonade in a dessert form with the addition of other spring favorites: strawberry pudding and fresh berries.

For the lemon pudding

½ cup + 1 tablespoon (135 ml) lemon juice

½ cup (115 g) mashed avocado

3 tablespoons (60 g) agave or coconut nectar

2 tablespoons (30 ml) melted coconut butter (page 32)

1 teaspoon packed lemon zest

3 drops stevia

2 pinches turmeric, for color

For the strawberry pudding

1½ cups (218 g) diced strawberries

1 tablespoon (15 ml) lemon juice

1½ tablespoons (30 g) agave or coconut nectar

½ cup (68 g) cashews

2 or 3 drops stevia

1½ tablespoons (22 ml) melted coconut oil

For assembly

2 cups (290 g) diced strawberries, for garnish

To make the lemon pudding Blend the lemon juice, avocado, and nectar until smooth in a blender. Add the coconut butter, lemon zest, stevia, and turmeric. Blend again. Chill the pudding for at least 4 hours.

To make the strawberry pudding Blend all ingredients but the coconut oil until smooth and creamy. Add the oil and blend again. Chill the pudding in the fridge for at least 4 hours.

To assemble Layer both puddings in glasses alone or with diced strawberries.

Yield 2 or 3 servings

banana brownie parfait

I love banana and chocolate together. There are lots of both of them in this parfait, with layers of maca brownie crumbles, chocolate banana pudding, and chopped bananas. I hope you enjoy it as much as I do.

To make the brownie Combine all ingredients in a food processor until crumbly. Processing any more will cause the brownie to become oily.

To make the pudding Blend the banana, cashews, maple syrup, cacao powder, and vanilla in a blender until completely smooth. Add the cacao butter and blend again to incorporate. Chill the pudding in the fridge for at least 5 hours.

To assemble Arrange some of the diced bananas in a glass. Spoon a layer of pudding on top and sprinkle some brownie mixture over it. Repeat the layers 1 or 2 more times. Serve immediately.

Yield 4 to 6 servings

For the brownie

1 cup (100 g) walnuts

⅔ cup (120 g) packed dates, chopped

2 tablespoons (11 g) cacao powder

1 tablespoon (9 g) maca powder

½ teaspoon vanilla bean powder

½ teaspoon water

For the pudding

1½ cups (338 g) mashed banana

⅔ cup (90 g) cashews

3 tablespoons (60 g) maple syrup

2 tablespoons (11 g) cacao powder

1 teaspoon vanilla bean powder

2 tablespoons (30 ml) melted cacao butter (page 23)

For assembly

2 or 3 ripe bananas, diced

chapter ten | **liquid desserts**

Sometimes it's nice to sip on dessert instead of eating it. These drinks will satisfy your sweet tooth and nourish your body. Smoothies are an easy way to get the nutrition that fruit, nuts, superfoods, and medicinal teas have to offer. Turn any of these smoothies into a meal when you're on the run and amp up the nutritional value by adding a handful of spinach or kale to it. Always consume smoothies immediately after making them.

Toast with a Caramel Apple Smoothie, page 150.

peanut butter and jelly smoothie

This smoothie is my favorite childhood sandwich in liquid form: peanut butter, jelly, and banana! The raw peanut butter tastes much different than the roasted kind. It's a little bitter, but it works so great with the sweetness of the other ingredients in the drink.

½ cup (120 ml) almond milk (page 30)

2 tablespoons (32 g) raw peanut butter (page 31)

1 large frozen banana

½ teaspoon vanilla extract

1 large date

2 large ice cubes, optional

¼ cup (80 g) berry jam (page 33)

Blend the milk, peanut butter, banana, vanilla, date, and ice cubes (if using) until smooth and creamy in a blender. Spoon most of the jam into the bottom of a glass and smear up the sides. Pour the smoothie in the glass. Swirl the last spoonful of jam into the top of the smoothie. Drink immediately.

Yield 1 serving

iced mocha

Despite the fact that this drink contains no coffee, I think it'll satisfy any coffee lover. Teeccino and a medicine flower extract give it a coffee flavor and the raw chocolate will give you an energy boost. It also doubles as a hot mocha. Just warm the drink in a pot over low on the stove and serve it in a mug.

Blend the almond milk, Teeccino, chocolate sauce, and coffee extract (if using) in a blender until frothy. Pour over ice cubes in a glass.

Yield 1 serving

TIP For an extra treat and a pretty presentation, drizzle more chocolate sauce inside the glass before pouring the drink in.

½ cup (120 ml) almond milk (page 30)

½ cup chilled Teeccino

2 tablespoons (30 g) chocolate sauce (page 32)

2 or 3 drops coffee medicine flower extract, optional

Ice cubes

chocolate superfood shake

This shake is nutritionally dense and tasty. Packed with superfoods and cacao, it's sure to keep you going for ages. For even longer-lasting energy add a frozen banana instead of the ice and omit the stevia.

½ to ⅔ cup (120 to 160 ml) almond milk (page 30)

3 tablespoons (26 g) cashews

2 tablespoons (11 g) cacao powder

1 tablespoon (9 g) maca powder

1 tablespoon (9 g) lucuma powder

2 teaspoons (6 g) chia seed

1 tablespoon (9 g) coconut sugar

1 tablespoon (7 g) hemp seeds

¼ teaspoon vanilla bean powder or vanilla extract

2 teaspoons (7 g) cacao nibs, optional

4 to 6 drops stevia

4 large ice cubes

Blend all but the ice in a high-speed blender until smooth. Add the ice and blend again briefly. Serve immediately.

Yield 1 serving

TIP Substitute the almond milk with chilled medicinal teas such as chaga, reishi, or pau d'arco.

creamy strawberry orange shake

This is a light and refreshing smoothie that is especially great during the hot summer months. The spirulina is optional but adds a great nutritional boost and creates a pretty two-toned presentation.

Blend the milk, juice, strawberries, vanilla, dates, and hemp seeds until smooth in a blender. Pour a few tablespoons of the smoothie into each glass and stir ¼ to ½ teaspoon spirulina (if using) into each one. Pour the remaining smoothie on top. Drink immediately.

Yield 2 servings

⅔ cup (160 ml) almond milk (page 30)

⅔ cup (160 ml) orange juice

2 cups (510 g) frozen diced strawberries

½ teaspoon vanilla extract or ½ teaspoon vanilla bean powder

2 large dates

1½ tablespoons (10 g) hemp seeds

½ to 1 teaspoon spirulina, optional

caramel apple smoothie

This smoothie is dessert in liquid form. Jazz it up by drizzling caramel sauce (page 33) on the inside of the glass before pouring the drink in and garnish it with a slice of apple.

1 tablespoon (10 g) chia seeds

½ cup (120 ml) almond milk (page 30)

1 large apple, peeled, cored, and chopped

1 tablespoon (16 g) almond butter

¾ teaspoon pure vanilla extract

2 tablespoons (9 g) lucuma powder

2 dates, pitted

4 or 5 drops caramel medicine flower extract, optional

4 or 5 large ice cubes

Soak the chia seeds in the almond milk in the blender while preparing the remaining ingredients. Blend all ingredients but the ice cubes in a high-speed blender until smooth. Add the ice and blend again until incorporated. Serve immediately.

Yield 1 or 2 servings

TIP To make this smoothie even more decadent, use frozen almond milk cubes in place of the ice cubes.

kiwi lime smoothie

This tasty green smoothie contains kiwi, which is high in vitamin C and fiber. The spinach also boosts the nutritional value and adds a bright green color. For instructions on cutting an avocado, see page 151.

½ cup (120 ml) almond milk (page 30)

1 kiwi, peeled and quartered

¼ cup (34 g) mashed avocado

2 large dates

¼ cup (50 ml) lime juice

1 handful spinach

4 or 5 large ice cubes

2 to 4 drops stevia, optional

Blend all ingredients but the ice and stevia until smooth and creamy in a blender. Add the ice and stevia (if using) and blend again. Add more lime juice if you want a tangier smoothie.

Yield 1 serving

how to **cut an avocado**

An avocado is ripe when it is slightly soft to the touch, especially at the top.

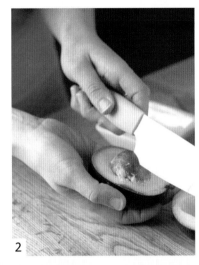

1. Holding the avocado with one hand and a knife in the other, make a cut into the avocado until the knife touches the pit and then move the knife all the way around the pit. Separate the avocado in half with your hands.

2. Tap the heel of a knife firmly into the pit.

3. Give it a wiggle and pull it out.

4. Holding one half in your hand, use the knife to score a crisscross pattern through the avocado flesh.

5. Spoon out the avocado chunks.

sweet and spicy hot chocolate

Yes, you can enjoy raw hot chocolate! This luscious drink can be gently warmed while maintaining its nutritional benefits. The cayenne and cinnamon add a tasty kick.

1⅓ cups (315 ml) almond milk (page 30)

¼ cup (38 g) coconut sugar

¼ cup (60 ml) melted coconut butter (page 32)

2½ tablespoons (13 g) cacao powder

½ teaspoon vanilla extract

1 teaspoon cinnamon

Few pinches cayenne pepper

Pinch Himalayan salt

Warm the almond milk over low heat on the stove until it is hot but you can comfortably stick a finger in it. Blend the hot milk and all other ingredients in a blender until combined and frothy. Serve immediately or warm it up a bit more on low heat on the stove.

Yield 2 servings

TIP For plain hot chocolate, omit the cinnamon and cayenne. For medicinal hot chocolate, substitute 1 cup (235 ml) of the almond milk for hot tea such as chaga or reishi.

butterscotch shake

This is a simple smoothie but it tastes like a combination of butterscotch and caramel. The butterscotch extract isn't necessary but it does boost the flavor a lot. Use maple syrup, to taste, in place of the stevia if desired.

Blend all ingredients in a high-speed blender until smooth. Serve immediately.

Yield 1 or 2 servings

²/₃ cup (160 ml) almond milk (page 30)

1 medium frozen banana

2 tablespoons (32 g) almond butter

2 tablespoons (9 g) lucuma powder

½ teaspoon vanilla extract

10 drops butterscotch medicine flower extract, optional

2 or 3 drops stevia

5 large ice cubes

carob-banana shake

Carob's natural sweetness works great with the banana and vanilla in this drink.

¾ cup (175 ml) almond milk, (page 30) or coconut milk, (page 30)

1 large frozen banana

3 tablespoons (19 g) carob powder

2 dates

½ teaspoon vanilla bean powder

2 large ice cubes

Blend all ingredients until smooth in a blender, adding enough milk for your desired consistency. Drink immediately.

Yield 1 or 2 servings

cherry-lime mint spritzer

Here's a refreshing spritzer without the alcohol. I like to sip on this often in the heat of summer.

Place a few ice cubes in each glass. Pour the lime juice, sparkling water, cherry extract, and stevia over the ice. Stir the ingredients together with a spoon. Stick a large sprig of mint into each glass. The flavor will quickly start to infuse. Drink immediately.

Yield 2 servings

Ice cubes

¼ cup (60 ml) lime juice

1 cup (235 ml) sparkling water

Cherry medicine flower extract, to taste

Stevia, to taste

Sprig of mint for each glass

resources

Raw Food Ingredients

USA

Medicine Flower, www.medicineflower.com
Raw Food World, www.therawfoodworld.com
Raw Guru, www.rawguru.com
Sprout Living, www.sproutliving.com
Sweet Leaf Stevia, www.sweetleaf.com
Vivapura, www.vivapura.com

Canada

Raw Nutrition, www.rawnutrition.ca
Truly Organic Foods, www.trulyorganicfoods.com
Upaya Naturals, www.upayanaturals.com

United Kingdom

Detox Your World, www.detoxyourworld.com

Australia

Conscious Choice, www.conscious-choice.com
Loving Earth, www.lovingearth.net
Raw Power, www.rawpower.com.au

Kitchen Equipment

Excalibur dehydrator, www.excaliburdehydrator.com
Vitamix blender, www.vitamix.com

Raw Food Blogs

Sweetly Raw, http://sweetlyraw.com
Chef Amber Shea, http://chefambershea.com
Choosing Raw, http://choosingraw.com
Fragrant Vanilla Cake,
    http://fragrantvanillacake.blogspot.ca
Raw Food Recipes,
    www.rawfoodrecipes.com
Raw Judita, http://rawjudita.blogspot.ca
Raw On $10 a Day, www.rawon10.com
The Raw Chef, www.therawchef.com
Vivapura Blog, blog.vivapura.com

Raw Food Schools and Courses

Indigo Food, Vancouver, BC, Canada
www.indigofood.org

Living Light, Fort Bragg, CA
www.rawfoodchef.com

Matthew Kenny Cuisine,
Santa Monica, CA, and New England
www.matthewkenneycuisine.com

The Raw Chef, Online Course
www.therawchef.com/courses/
chef-homestudy-sp

Raw Foundation, Vancouver, BC, Canada
www.rawfoodfoundation.org

Raw Food Books

Ani's Raw Food Essentials: Recipes and Techniques for Mastering the Art of Live Food, Ani Phyo

Easy Affordable Raw: How to Go Raw on $10 a Day, Lisa Viger

Everyday Raw Express: Recipes in 30 Minutes or Less, Matthew Kenney

Going Raw: Everything You Need to Start Your Own Raw Food Diet and Lifestyle Revolution at Home, Judita Wignall

Practically Raw: Flexible Recipes Anyone Can Make, Amber Shea Crawley

Raw and Simple: Eat Well and Live Radiantly with 100 Truly Quick and Easy Recipes for the Raw Food Lifestyle, Judita Wignall

about the author

Heather Pace became a health-conscious vegan at the age of fourteen after reading the book *Fit for Life* by Harvey and Marilyn Diamond. She discovered new ways to enjoy her favorite foods, particularly her beloved desserts. Heather's curiosity was piqued when she stumbled upon a raw food restaurant at the age of sixteen, and by the time she was eighteen, she had attended her first month-long raw food retreat.

Heather's passion for food led her to a two-year classical culinary school program where she gained valuable knowledge and experience. She went on to work in various restaurants and bakeries, and as a personal chef. Heather has authored seven raw vegan dessert e-books and teaches raw food classes internationally. She is the founder of Sweetly Raw, www.sweetlyraw.com, a resource for more raw food recipes and a community for those who are interested in raw food cooking.

Heather is also a certified Kripalu yoga instructor and a keen world traveler.

acknowledgments

Biggest thanks to my mom who set my whole natural-food passion in motion by giving me the book *Fit for Life* to read when I was fourteen. Thank you for always encouraging me to follow my heart and live out my dreams. Thanks to my friends and family who have supported me and have always believed in me. And of course, thanks for taste testing my food all these years.

Thank you to Quarry Books for giving me this opportunity to bring my recipes into the world.

Huge thanks to Melissa Welsh and to our assistants, Natasha, Meridith, and Tyler. It was so much fun to work together.

And more thanks to Excalibur, Vivapura, and Medicine Flower Essences for donating supplies.

about the photographer

Melissa Welsh is an award-winning photographer who lives in Nelson, British Columbia. She is a fun, free-spirited individual with a deep love for adventure. Her work can be found in private collections around the world as well as in regional, national, and international publications. She currently serves as the national communications chair for the Professional Photographers of Canada. See more of her work at www.melissawelsh.com.

index